In Dreams Together

THE AZRIELI SERIES OF HOLOCAUST SURVIVOR MEMOIRS: PUBLISHED TITLES

ENGLISH TITLES

Judy Abrams, *Tenuous Threads/* Eva Felsen-
 burg Marx, *One of the Lucky Ones*
Amek Adler, *Six Lost Years*
Ferenc Andai, *In the Hour of Fate and
 Danger*
Molly Applebaum, *Buried Words: The Diary
 of Molly Applebaum*
Claire Baum, *The Hidden Package*
Bronia and Joseph Beker, *Joy Runs Deeper*
Tibor Benyovits, *Unsung Heroes*
Max Bornstein, *If Home Is Not Here*
Felicia Carmelly, *Across the Rivers of Memory*
Judy Cohen, *A Cry in Unison*
Tommy Dick, *Getting Out Alive*
Marian Domanski, *Fleeing from the Hunter*
Anita Ekstein, *Always Remember Who You
 Are*
John Freund, *Spring's End*
Susan Garfield, *Too Many Goodbyes: The
 Diaries of Susan Garfield*
Myrna Goldenberg (Editor), *Before All
 Memory Is Lost: Women's Voices from the
 Holocaust*
René Goldman, *A Childhood Adrift*
Elly Gotz, *Flights of Spirit*
Ibolya Grossman and Andy Réti, *Stronger
 Together*
Pinchas Gutter, *Memories in Focus*
Anna Molnár Hegedűs, *As the Lilacs Bloomed*
Rabbi Pinchas Hirschprung, *The Vale of Tears*
Bronia Jablon, *A Part of Me*
Helena Jockel, *We Sang in Hushed Voices*
Eddie Klein, *Inside the Walls*
Michael Kutz, *If, By Miracle*
Ferenc Laczó (Editor), *Confronting Devasta-
 tion: Memoirs of Holocaust Survivors
 from Hungary*

Nate Leipciger, *The Weight of Freedom*
Alex Levin, *Under the Yellow and
 Red Stars*
Rachel Lisogurski and Chana Broder,
 Daring to Hope
Fred Mann, *A Drastic Turn of Destiny*
Michael Mason, *A Name Unbroken*
Leslie Meisels with Eva Meisels, *Suddenly
 the Shadow Fell*
Leslie Mezei, *A Tapestry of Survival*
Muguette Myers, *Where Courage Lives*
David Newman, *Hope's Reprise*
Arthur Ney, *W Hour*
Felix Opatowski, *Gatehouse to Hell*
Marguerite Élias Quddus, *In Hiding*
Maya Rakitova, *Behind the Red Curtain*
Henia Reinhartz, *Bits and Pieces*
Betty Rich, *Little Girl Lost*
Paul-Henri Rips, *E/96: Fate Undecided*
Margrit Rosenberg Stenge, *Silent Refuge*
Steve Rotschild, *Traces of What Was*
Judith Rubinstein, *Dignity Endures*
Martha Salcudean, *In Search of Light*
Kitty Salsberg and Ellen Foster,
 Never Far Apart
Joseph Schwarzberg, *Dangerous Measures*
Zuzana Sermer, *Survival Kit*
Rachel Shtibel, *The Violin/* Adam Shtibel,
 A Child's Testimony
Maxwell Smart, *Chaos to Canvas*
Gerta Solan, *My Heart Is At Ease*
Zsuzsanna Fischer Spiro, *In Fragile
 Moments/* Eva Shainblum,
 The Last Time
George Stern, *Vanished Boyhood*
Willie Sterner, *The Shadows Behind Me*
Ann Szedlecki, *Album of My Life*

William Tannenzapf, *Memories from the Abyss*/ Renate Krakauer, *But I Had a Happy Childhood*

Elsa Thon, *If Only It Were Fiction*

Agnes Tomasov, *From Generation to Generation*

Joseph Tomasov, *From Loss to Liberation*

Sam Weisberg, *Carry the Torch*/ Johnny Jablon, *A Lasting Legacy*

Leslie Vertes, *Alone in the Storm*

Anka Voticky, *Knocking on Every Door*

TITRES FRANÇAIS

Judy Abrams, *Retenue par un fil*/ Eva Felsenburg Marx, *Une question de chance*

Molly Applebaum, *Les Mots enfouis: Le Journal de Molly Applebaum*

Claire Baum, *Le Colis caché*

Bronia et Joseph Beker, *Plus forts que le malheur*

Max Bornstein, *Citoyen de nulle part*

Tommy Dick, *Objectif: survivre*

Marian Domanski, *Traqué*

John Freund, *La Fin du printemps*

Myrna Goldenberg (Éditrice), *Un combat singulier: Femmes dans la tourmente de l'Holocauste*

René Goldman, *Une enfance à la dérive*

Anna Molnár Hegedűs, *Pendant la saison des lilas*

Helena Jockel, *Nous chantions en sourdine*

Michael Kutz, *Si, par miracle*

Nate Leipciger, *Le Poids de la liberté*

Alex Levin, *Étoile jaune, étoile rouge*

Fred Mann, *Un terrible revers de fortune*

Michael Mason, *Au fil d'un nom*

Leslie Meisels, *Soudain, les ténèbres*

Muguette Myers, *Les Lieux du courage*

Arthur Ney, *L'Heure W*

Felix Opatowski, *L'Antichambre de l'enfer*

Marguerite Élias Quddus, *Cachée*

Henia Reinhartz, *Fragments de ma vie*

Betty Rich, *Seule au monde*

Paul-Henri Rips, *Matricule E/96*

Steve Rotschild, *Sur les traces du passé*

Kitty Salsberg et Ellen Foster, *Unies dans l'épreuve*

Zuzana Sermer, *Trousse de survie*

Rachel Shtibel, *Le Violon*/ Adam Shtibel, *Témoignage d'un enfant*

George Stern, *Une jeunesse perdue*

Willie Sterner, *Les Ombres du passé*

Ann Szedlecki, *L'Album de ma vie*

William Tannenzapf, *Souvenirs de l'abîme*/ Renate Krakauer, *Le Bonheur de l'innocence*

Elsa Thon, *Que renaisse demain*

Agnes Tomasov, *De génération en génération*

Leslie Vertes, *Seul dans la tourmente*

Anka Voticky, *Frapper à toutes les portes*

In Dreams Together:
The Diary of Leslie Fazekas

Leslie Fazekas

THE AZRIELI FOUNDATION · www.azrielifoundation.org

Cover and book design by Mark Goldstein
Translation of the diary and letters of Leslie Fazekas from Hungarian by Péter Balikó Lengyel (2020), except where noted. Translation reviewed by Marietta Morry and Lynda Muir
Pages 82–85, 91–96 and 105–113 in the memoir of Leslie Fazekas translated from Hungarian by Marietta Morry and Lynda Muir (2018)
Annotations in diary, letters and memoir provided by László Csősz
Photo on page 145 courtesy of the Hungarian National Museum. Maps on pages xxxviii–xxxix by Deborah Crowle. Endpaper maps by Martin Gilbert

LIBRARY AND ARCHIVES CANADA CATALOGUING IN PUBLICATION

In dreams together: the diary of Leslie Fazekas / Leslie Fazekas.

Fazekas, Leslie, 1925– author. Azrieli Foundation, publisher.
The Azrieli series of Holocaust survivor memoirs; XII
    Translated from the Hungarian; original title unknown.
    Includes bibliographical references and index.
ISBN 9781988065694 (softcover) · Canadiana 20200400452 · 8 7 6 5 4 3 2 1

LCSH: Fazekas, Leslie, 1925– — Diaries. LCSH: Holocaust survivors — Hungary — Debrecen — Biography. LCSH: Jews — Hungary — Debrecen — Biography. LCSH: Immigrants — Canada — Biography. LCGFT: Diaries. LCGFT: Autobiographies.

LCC DS135.H93 F39 2020 · DDC 940.53/18092 — dc23

The Azrieli Foundation's Holocaust Survivor Memoirs Program

Naomi Azrieli, Publisher

Jody Spiegel, Program Director
Arielle Berger, Managing Editor
Catherine Person, Manager and Editor of French Translations
Catherine Aubé, Editor of French Translations
Matt Carrington, Editor
Devora Levin, Editor and Special Projects Coordinator
Stephanie Corazza, Historian and Manager of Academic Initiatives
Marc-Olivier Cloutier, Manager of Education Initiatives
Elin Beaumont, Community and Education Initiatives
Elizabeth Banks, Digital Asset Curator and Archivist

Mark Goldstein, Art Director
Bruno Paradis, Layout, French-Language Editions

Contents

Series Preface:
In their own words. . .

In telling these stories, the writers have liberated themselves. For so many years we did not speak about it, even when we became free people living in a free society. Now, when at last we are writing about what happened to us in this dark period of history, knowing that our stories will be read and live on, it is possible for us to feel truly free. These unique historical documents put a face on what was lost, and allow readers to grasp the enormity of what happened to six million Jews — one story at a time.

David J. Azrieli, C.M., C.Q., M.Arch
Holocaust survivor and founder, The Azrieli Foundation

Since the end of World War II, approximately 40,000 Jewish Holocaust survivors have immigrated to Canada. Who they are, where they came from, what they experienced and how they built new lives for themselves and their families are important parts of our Canadian heritage. The Azrieli Foundation's Holocaust Survivor Memoirs Program was established in 2005 to preserve and share the memoirs written by those who survived the twentieth-century Nazi genocide of the Jews of Europe and later made their way to Canada. The memoirs encourage readers to engage thoughtfully and critically with the complexities of the Holocaust and to create meaningful connections with the lives of survivors.

Millions of individual stories are lost to us forever. By preserving the stories written by survivors and making them widely available to a broad audience, the Azrieli Foundation's Holocaust Survivor Memoirs Program seeks to sustain the memory of all those who perished at the hands of hatred, abetted by indifference and apathy. The personal accounts of those who survived against all odds are as different as the people who wrote them, but all demonstrate the courage, strength, wit and luck that it took to prevail and survive in such terrible adversity. The memoirs are also moving tributes to people — strangers and friends — who risked their lives to help others, and who, through acts of kindness and decency in the darkest of moments, frequently helped the persecuted maintain faith in humanity and courage to endure. These accounts offer inspiration to all, as does the survivors' desire to share their experiences so that new generations can learn from them.

The Holocaust Survivor Memoirs Program collects, archives and publishes select survivor memoirs and makes the print editions available free of charge to educational institutions and Holocaust-education programs across Canada. They are also available for sale online to the general public. All revenues to the Azrieli Foundation from the sales of the Azrieli Series of Holocaust Survivor Memoirs go toward the publishing and educational work of the memoirs program.

~

The Azrieli Foundation would like to express appreciation to the following people for their invaluable efforts in producing this book: Doris Bergen, Jean-Philippe Bouriette, JoAnne Burek, László Csősz, Mark Duffus (Maracle Inc.), Farla Klaiman, Susan Roitman, and Margie Wolfe & Emma Rodgers of Second Story Press.

About the Footnotes and Glossary

The following memoir contains a number of terms, concepts and historical references that may be unfamiliar to the reader. English translations of foreign-language words and terms have been added to the text. Footnotes have been provided to add relevant background information and references to a number of quotations. For general information on major organizations, significant historical events and people, geographical locations, religious and cultural terms, and foreign-language words and expressions that will help give context and background to the events described in the text, please see the glossary beginning on page 131.

Introduction

The destruction of the Hungarian Jewish communities in the last phase
of World War II was one of the most efficient genocidal campaigns
in history. In March 1944, some 750,000 Jews living in Hungary represented by far the largest surviving community in Hitler's Europe.
With the imminent defeat of the Nazis approaching, they had good
reason to believe their sufferings would be over soon. However, following the German occupation of Hungary that very month, the
Nazis and their local accomplices completed the disenfranchisement, plunder and isolation of the Jews in a period of a mere eight
weeks. Then, mostly between mid-May and early July 1944, the Nazi
and Hungarian authorities deported about 450,000 people from the
Hungarian provinces. Their destination was the Auschwitz-Birkenau
camp complex, where three-fourths of them were gassed upon arrival, killing more than 300,000 people: mainly women, children and
the elderly. It was due to the Hungarian campaign — *Ungarnaktion*,
as the Nazi jargon put it — that Auschwitz ultimately became the
universally known symbol of human genocide. In the words of the
towering Holocaust scholar Raul Hilberg, "Hungary was going to lift
Auschwitz to the top" among other Nazi camps.[1]

---

1 Raul Hilberg, "Auschwitz and the 'Final Solution,'" in *Anatomy of the Auschwitz
Death Camp*, eds. Yisrael Gutman and Michael Berenbaum (Bloomington: Indi-
ana University Press in association with the USHMM, 1998), 88.

It is a less well-known fact, however, that some 3 per cent of the deported Hungarian Jews actually escaped being sent to Birkenau. At the end of June 1944, more than 15,000 people were transported to the Vienna region (*Gau Groß-Wien*), in Nazi-annexed Austria, rather than to the death camp. Moreover, they were indeed taken there primarily for work purposes. Arriving at the distribution camp (*Durchgangslager*) in Strasshof, the Jews were transferred to various districts of Vienna and settlements in the vicinity, where they worked in different branches of war industry and in agriculture, as well as at rubble clean-up and construction sites. Those unable to work were not murdered, and families were mostly allowed to stay together. Living conditions, workload and treatment varied, but at large, the situation of Hungarian Jewish slave labourers in and around Vienna was relatively bearable, if compared to the extreme sufferings in other corners in the web of Nazi concentration and labour camps. Many of the deportees in Austria fell victim to bomb raids, accidents, illnesses, hardships and arbitrary executions, but eventually the majority of this group, an estimated ten to twelve thousand people, survived the war. The author of these outstanding wartime diaries and postwar memoir, László Frenkel, today Leslie Fazekas, was among them.

This specific sub-chapter of the Holocaust in Hungary has several ramifications, which are intertwined with various debated fields of Holocaust scholarship and remembrance, including the assessment of the activities of Jewish leadership during the Holocaust, Nazi-Zionist negotiations, postwar justice, the roles of local perpetrators and "bystanders" and many other issues. In historical texts, scholars commonly refer to this area of the Holocaust as the "Strasshof rescue operation" or "putting Jews on ice."[2] Both terms are slightly misleading, however. Despite their genocidal aims, in the last phase of the war the Nazis also urgently needed to obtain a workforce for military

---

2 Randolph L. Braham, *The Politics of Genocide: The Holocaust in Hungary*, 3rd ed. (Boulder: Columbia University Press, 2016), 850–854. József Schiller, *A strasshofi mentőakció története és előzményei* [*The History and Antecedents of the Strasshof Rescue Action*] (Budapest: Cserépfalvi, 1996.)

production. Thousands of industrial and construction companies, farms and infrastructural projects required cheap slave labour of prisoners of war and civil forced labourers, including Jews.

The decision to send Jewish labourers to Austria is generally believed to have been the consequence of the infamous negotiations between SS-*Obersturmbannführer* Adolf Eichmann, one of the main architects of the "Final Solution," and a group of Hungarian Zionists. In fact, there was only an indirect link between the two series of events.

The Budapest Relief and Rescue Committee (also known by its abbreviated Hebrew name, *Va'ada*) was an underground body, established in early 1943 with the support of international Jewish organizations, aiming at coordinating Zionist activities to support Jewish refugees in Hungary. Following the Nazi invasion, they wasted no time to find ways to thwart the impending destruction or at least to save some lives. Their strategy also included negotiations with German and Hungarian authorities. The most difficult and controversial task fell on lawyer and journalist Rezső (Rudolf) Kasztner and his associates. They attempted to negotiate with Adolf Eichmann's *Sondereinsatzkommando*, the special force in charge of the deportations. Their efforts were unexpectedly supported by a turn of international high politics. SS leader Heinrich Himmler, facing impending defeat, was seeking a separate peace agreement with the Western Allies, behind Adolf Hitler's back. Through his representatives in Hungary, he made his infamous offer to exchange "blood for goods": the lives of one million European Jews for military equipment and large amounts of consumable goods. British and American leaders never even considered the deal.[3]

---

3 For further details about the 1944 activities and negotiations of the Rescue Committee, including the Kasztner case, see Braham, *The Politics of Genocide,* Chapter 29; Yehuda Bauer, *Jews for Sale? Nazi-Jewish Negotiations, 1933–1945* (New Haven–London: Yale University Press, 1994), 172–209; Zoltán Vági, László Csősz and Gábor Kádár, *The Holocaust in Hungary: Evolution of a Genocide* (Lanham, MD–Washington, DC: AltaMira Press–USHMM, 2013), 265–272.

However, in the wake of the failed operation, Kasztner could continue the negotiations on a far smaller scale with SS-*Obersturmbannführer* Kurt Becher, Himmler's economic envoy to Hungary. In exchange for a sizable sum (1,000 USD per person),[4] a privileged group of close to 1,700 people was allowed to leave the territory of the Third Reich. Passengers included Kasztner's own family and friends, many other Zionists, refugees, children and prominent community members, including rabbis, artists, writers, bankers and industrialists. The so-called "Kasztner train" left Budapest on June 30, 1944, for a special section constructed inside the Bergen-Belsen concentration camp. Its passengers ultimately reached safety in neutral Switzerland in two groups in August and December 1944.

While the Nazi-Zionist negotiations were going on, in early June, the Nazi governor (*Gauleiter*) of the Vienna district requested workers for projects of "military importance" in the region from Ernst Kaltenbrunner, the head of the Reich Main Security Office (RSHA).[5] Kaltenbrunner instructed Eichmann to send some transports to Vienna a couple of days later, which came as a godsend for Eichmann, who could present this as a concession in his ongoing negotiations with Kasztner on June 14.[6] The Strasshof deportations probably would have taken place even if Eichmann had not been in contact with Kasztner and the Zionists. However, later on both the "Kasztner

---

4   Equal to roughly 15,000 USD today.

5   Randolph L. Braham, ed., *The Destruction of Hungarian Jewry: A Documentary Account*, 2 vols. (New York: Pro Arte for the World Federation of Hungarian Jews, 1963), vol. 2, document 184, pp. 415–416.

6   Eichmann offered to put 30,000 Hungarian Jews "on ice" in exchange for administrative "expenses" (meaning ransom paid to his coffers). The Zionist organization agreed to pay 100 USD per person "if the Jews remained alive." Ultimately, a contingent of only 15,000 Jews were directed to Austria. Rezső Kasztner, eds. László Karsai and Judit Molnár, *The Kasztner Report: The Report of the Budapest Jewish Rescue Committee, 1942–1945* (Jerusalem: Yad Vashem, 2013), 146–147.

Jews" and the Hungarian Jewish slave labourers in Austria were su-
pervised by the Vienna branch of the German Security Police (Si-
cherheitspolizei), under the leadership of Adolf Eichmann's deputy,
SS-*Obersturmbannführer* Hermann Krumey. It suggests that both
groups were in the status of the "special hostages" of the SS.

According to the "master plan" of the deportations, Hungary was
divided into six zones along the regional division of the gendarmerie,
which was one of the key agents in the process. Hungarian and German authorities emptied zones one by one, with lightning speed. On
June 16, they started the liquidation of ghettos in Deportation Zone
IV, Eastern Hungary, including the major cities of Debrecen and Szeged. Due to the timing of the request from Kaltenbrunner, the special
transports directed to Austria were to be selected from the transit
camps of this region. According to the statistics provided by a young
Hungarian Jewish woman, who was forced to work for the SS office
at the distribution camp of Strasshof, they registered 15,011 people
from transit camps in the provinces, including two transports from
Debrecen (6,641 people) and Szeged (5,239), and one each from Szolnok (2,567) and Baja (564), as well as 1,690 people arriving on the
"Kasztner train."[7]

The main cohort of deportees arrived from Debrecen, hometown
of László Frenkel and his family. Debrecen was the second largest
city in Hungary during the interwar years and remains so today. The
economic and cultural centre of Eastern Hungary, it was a mostly
Protestant city, in a country dominated by Catholicism. During the
war years, the city had more than 125,000 inhabitants, including
some 9,500 Jews (7.5 per cent). The overwhelming majority of the
population was ethnic Hungarian and almost exclusively Hungarian-
speaking. László Frenkel's family belonged to the Status Quo Ante

---

7 Hungarian Jewish Museum and Archives, testimony of Edit Csillag, DEGOB
   Protocols, no. 3628.

community, a unique branch of Judaism that only 5 per cent of the Jews in Hungary followed but that dominated in Debrecen.[8] The traditional Jewish neighbourhood in the city started to develop in the middle of the nineteenth century from the streets running southwest of the city's main square, between the then Nagy Hatvan and the Széchenyi streets. Symbolizing their social status, economic power and integration, at the very end of the nineteenth century the Status Quo community built a magnificent two-towered synagogue on the main street. Another Status Quo synagogue had existed in the Jewish district, along with the Orthodox synagogue and several community buildings, including the Jewish Grammar School, which were in close proximity with the house in Széchenyi Street that was one of the Frenkel family's home during the 1930s.

In 1925, Hungary witnessed a period of political and social consolidation following the lost war, the collapse of the Austro-Hungarian Monarchy, traumatic territorial losses, and an era of rampaging political violence between 1918 and 1921. The authoritarian and antiliberal regime of Admiral Miklós Horthy started its reign with antisemitic retaliatory measures and a discriminatory law that drastically limited the number of Jews permitted to enrol in higher education.[9] From the early 1920s on, however, the government followed a more lenient policy, due to economic and foreign policy considerations.

---

8 The expression *status quo ante* (Latin: "the way things were before") refers to the Great Schism of Judaism in Hungary (1868–69), when the Israelite Congress decided to split the community into two branches, the modernist Neolog and the traditionalist Orthodox. "Status Quo" was a small faction that joined neither of the new communities but followed more traditional ways. See Jacob Katz, *A House Divided: Orthodoxy and Schism in Nineteenth-Century Central European Jewry* (Waltham, MA: Brandeis University Press, 1998).

9 The so-called Numerus Clausus Law, Act XXV of 1920.

For a while it seemed the relations of Jews and non-Jews could return to normality and liberal-era equality. However, antisemitic sentiments and implicitly anti-Jewish practices lingered on. The economic crisis of the early 1930s hit Hungary hard, brought about another right-wing political turn and gradually radicalized the political climate. These changes were of course fostered by the rise and growing successes of Nazism.

In 1935, at the age of ten, László continued his studies in the Jewish Grammar School (*Gymnasium*) in Debrecen. He had no other real choice: although not prescribed by law, local secondary schools discriminated against Jewish pupils, and therefore, in 1921, the Jewish community had been forced to establish a segregated school exclusively for Jewish children, who had previously attended state-run or church schools. László and his schoolmates were growing up in an ever-darkening political atmosphere. The years of 1938 to 1942 witnessed the gradual escalation of antisemitic policies, which soon directly affected the everyday lives of their families. The Hungarian state adopted new anti-Jewish laws, which deprived Jewish citizens of their civil rights and opportunities. The first two laws were primarily aimed at economic and social positions, whereas the third law was modelled on Nazi racial laws, forbidding marriages and sexual relations between Jews and non-Jews. The laws brought about general impoverishment, especially among the middle and lower-middle classes. At least ninety thousand people lost their jobs.

With Hungary joining the war, their lives were at stake as well. Hungarian authorities pursued increasingly radical anti-minority policies, especially in the territories Hungary regained with Nazi support, and committed atrocities that culminated in the deportation of some 20,000 Jews, including refugees from Nazi-occupied countries, but also Hungarian citizens in the summer of 1941. These people were driven to former Soviet territories, where most of them were murdered by the SS.[10] At the same time, Hungarian Jewish men were labelled collectively unreliable and were forced to perform unarmed auxiliary labour service in the army. They perished on the Eastern Front by the thousands due to harsh circumstances and events of the war, but also due to maltreatment by their Hungarian guards. During the momentous year of 1942, however, the "Jewish policy" of the Hungarian government underwent a significant change.

Despite hardships and painful losses of lives in labour service, Debrecen Jews could live in peace and relative normalcy, compared to the fate of millions of Jews brutally persecuted and murdered in Hitler's Europe. The Nazis and their strong Hungarian supporters had demanded the Hungarian government take part in the "solution of the Jewish question" and expel the Jewish communities. However, the Hungarian government refused the demands, mostly for political concerns. As the chances for an Axis victory diminished, Hungary initiated negotiations for a separate truce with the Western Powers in 1943, and they intended to demonstrate their independence from the Nazi Empire with a more lenient "Jewish policy." The government made some mitigating gestures toward the Jewish community, which

---

10 Revising the terms of the post-World War I peace treaty was the prime motivation of Hungary to become an ally of Italy and Nazi Germany in the late 1930s and to fight on the side of the Axis powers during World War II. In four stages between 1938 and 1941, Hungary regained about 40 per cent of the territories it had lost to neighbouring countries, most prominently to Czechoslovakia, Romania and Yugoslavia. However, the territorial gains were obtained at the cost of entering the war. In November 1940, Hungary joined the Axis alliance, and then in June 1941, the Nazi invasion of the Soviet Union. In the newly annexed areas, Hungarian authorities launched a series of radical actions against local Jews. The 1941 expulsion of Jews with "unsettled citizenship" from Carpatho-Ruthenia and the 1942 raid in the Southern Province both resulted in mass murder. Such actions served as precursors to similar operations in Hungary proper in 1944. The peace treaty signed in Paris in 1947 re-established Hungary's pre-1938 borders with minor modifications.

caused a kind of cautious optimism.[11] At the end of 1943, when László fell in love with Judit Felbermann, there was every prospect that the war and the hardships of their families could end soon.

However, this state of affairs changed overnight on March 19, 1944. The Germans, who had been well aware of the "secret" peace talks, wanted to prevent Hungary from extricating itself from the war and therefore occupied the "unwilling satellite." Complying with German pressure, Regent Miklós Horthy appointed a new government consisting of well-known pro-Nazi political figures. Over the next two months, the Hungarian administration completed the marking, isolation and disenfranchisement of the Jewish citizens, as well as the expropriation of most of their property and their concentration in designated residential areas in the entire country, except Budapest. Nazi authorities took a lead in the anti-Jewish campaign, but they mostly left the implementation to the Hungarians. Adolf Eichmann's special force installed outposts in each major city to closely supervise the process. In Debrecen, the commander of the Security Police was SS-*Hauptsturmführer* Siegfried Seidl, who later also served at the Vienna branch of the *Sondereinsatzkommando*, which oversaw the camps of Hungarian Jewish labourers taken to Strasshof.[12]

The ghetto for the Debrecen Jews was set up in the middle of May

---

11 For example, the government allowed limited Jewish emigration to Palestine, and certain members of the Jewish elite still held important political and economic positions. See Braham, ed., *The Destruction of Hungarian Jewry*, documents 99 to 101.

12 Siegfried Seidl (1911–1947) was one of the closest associates of Adolf Eichmann. He was notorious as the commander of the Theresienstadt ghetto (1941–1943) and a leading functionary of the Bergen-Belsen camp (1943–1944). After the war, the Austrian People's Court convicted him for war crimes; he was sentenced to death and executed. For further details about his career, see Tomáš Fedorovič, "Der Theresienstädter Lagerkommandant Siegfried Seidl," in *Theresienstädter Studien und Dokumente*, (Hgs.) Jaroslava Milotová, Ulf Rathgeber, Michael Wögerbauer, Vol. 10 (Prag: Sefer-Verlag, 2003), 162–209.

in the traditional Jewish quarter, where some 50 per cent of the apartments were Jewish-owned property. Non-Jewish tenants had to leave the territory of the ghetto and were moved to former "Jewish" apartments. Initially, four square metres of living space was designated per person in the ghetto — that is, three to five people shared one room. However, the territory of the ghetto was soon reduced as a consequence of a major U S A F air raid on June 2, which caused a serious housing shortage in the city.

Jews spent about one month in the ghettos in Debrecen and its vicinity. The local authorities and the police in Debrecen treated the Jews in a relatively humane way, compared to the often ruthless methods of state representatives elsewhere. Starting on June 16, Hungarian gendarmerie transferred the more than 13,000 inhabitants of the ghettos in Debrecen and its surrounding areas (Hajdú County) to a central transit camp designated in a brickyard on the outskirts of Debrecen. Some people could find shelter in the buildings of the brickyard, but most of them were forced to stay in drying sheds without walls, or even under the open sky. The camp lacked even basic sanitary facilities, except for some makeshift latrines. The scarcity of water and food supplies made the situation unbearable after one or two days. Gendarme cadet corps from another part of the country took over command from local authorities and treatment significantly worsened. The young gendarmes would beat people with rubber batons, humiliate them and routinely rob them of their last personal belongings. A special inspection team of the gendarmerie brutally interrogated and tortured many Jews who were accused of trying to hide their personal belongings sequestrated by the state. Some Jews were killed or died by suicide during these ordeals.

The Jewish community was deported from Debrecen between June 25 and 28, 1944. The destination of three transports was the Auschwitz-Birkenau death camp. However, two other transports, carrying slightly more than half of the camp inmates (close to 6,700 people), were directed to Austria. The circumstances of deportation were equally cruel. One Strasshof survivor, sixteen-year-old Márta Balázs, remembered the brutality of the gendarmes like this:

...And then in the midst of great yelling, they pushed and crammed us into a cattle car, 80 people into a space that would at best have fit 40. This meant that we would be sitting on our packages, would pull our legs underneath us. Those who ended up at the wall of the cattle car were the luckiest, for they could at least prop their backs against it. We young people mostly ended up in the middle of the cattle car and propped our backs against one another's, in order to find a position that was more bearable to hold for days on end. We were given a bucket of water and a toilet bucket; the latter was a normal-sized pail that was supposed to serve the bodily needs of 80 people. There was grating on the windows, and an open crack of just a few inches was left on the door when it was then locked. And all this was in the midst of the June heat. One was suffocating from the lack of air, from thirst....[13]

The transport taking László Frenkel and his family members, as well as Judit Felbermann (also spelled as Felberman) and her family, took about two days to cover the nearly five hundred kilometres from Debrecen to Strasshof. The other train, however, was first directed to Auschwitz, probably due to a logistical mistake of the SS administration, and was turned back from the Kassa (Košice) border station. This way the journey lasted much longer, claiming several lives. As twelve-year-old Agnes Kaposi recounted the experience: "Our train stopped, as it had done countless times through our interminable journey. Four days and five nights with almost no water. People were dazed. Some were raving. I thought I was hallucinating when the wagon door opened. Someone barked: Wieviel Tod?! How many

---

13 Memoirs of Márta Balázs, undated (postwar). USHMM Archives RG 10.207, 36–37.

dead?! A relief: we were not in Hungary anymore. In our wagon there were two dead."[14]

As preparation for the Strasshof transports' compilation, local Jewish leaders were assigned the dreadful task of dividing the residents of the transit camps into two groups. Following a method well-tested in a host of other countries in earlier years of the war, right after the occupation of Hungary, Nazi and Hungarian authorities established Jewish councils (Judenräte), which were made responsible for the internal and administrative affairs of the community. In practice, this unwanted and tragic task involved the implementation of the orders of the authorities and the enforcement of the increasingly restrictive measures against the Jews. The selection process in the transit camp was accompanied by dramatic scenes. Based on the directives from the Central Jewish Council, it was primarily the prominent members of the congregations and their family members who could be placed into the "privileged" group, along with doctors, engineers and other specialists. Some well-known figures were listed separately. The remaining slots were supposed to be filled by those fit to work and family members of labour servicemen. Because most of the camp residents belonged in the latter two categories, there were difficulties with making the decision about whom to include. Jews had no specific information regarding the destinations, or the fate that was awaiting them there, but many suspected that the members of the first group would arrive at better circumstances.

After the end of the war, legal proceedings were initiated against Jewish leaders who were forced to make those fateful decisions. Tragically, several survivors blamed them for the loss of their loved ones. Another round of proceedings against certain Jewish camp functionaries — including camp doctors, foremen and members of the Jewish police (*Jupo*) — followed, which reflected the bitter internal

---

14 Agnes Kaposi, *Yellow Star, Red Star* (Manchester: I2i Publishing, 2020), 121.

conflicts that occasionally emerged among the prisoners. The nearly extinguished communities in Eastern Hungary were deeply divided by these issues. Despite the fact that ultimately none of the Jewish defendants were found guilty, the procedures clearly meant an additional trauma for the mentally and physically broken survivors.[15]

Another dividing line lay between those returning from the labour camps in Austria and other survivors. Members of the first group had to encounter an ambivalent situation: in spite of trauma and losses, their persecution was considered of "secondary" importance if compared to the horrors of Auschwitz and the other concentration camps. Since then, the deportations to Austria have remained a forgotten tragedy, shadowed by the magnitude of the massacre of more than 300,000 Hungarian Jews in Auschwitz-Birkenau as well as the mass experience of labour service and the ordeals of the Budapest community, both claiming tens of thousands of lives. Paradoxically, the specific experience of forced labour in Austria often contributed to postwar conflicts and raised antisemitic sentiments. The relatively "large" number of survivors in this region of Hungary (an estimated 35 to 40 per cent versus 10 to 20 per cent in other provinces outside of Budapest, where entire communities were deported to Auschwitz-Birkenau) fostered myths surrounding the returning survivors, myths represented by highly defamatory statements such as "more of them have returned than were deported."

Strasshof survivors were glaringly underrepresented in the postwar testimony projects and early memoir literature in the 1940s. During the period of the Soviet-style dictatorship, the official memory of the persecution of Jews in general was pushed into oblivion. With relative political consolidation in the 1960s, Holocaust-related scholarly

---

15 In Debrecen, at least ten legal proceedings were initiated against Holocaust survivors on these grounds. National Archives of Hungary, Hajdú-Bihar County Archives, RG x x v.1. and x x v, 22. b. 1945–1948.

and literary publications were permitted again, although selectively. The first major attempt to commemorate the Strasshof deportations, which gained considerable publicity, was a documentary novel in 1974 (Mária Ember, *Hajtűkanyar* [*Hairpin Bend*]), soon followed by other memoirs (Pál Bárdos, *Az első évtized* [*The First Decade*], 1975). The first scholarly efforts to analyze the events appeared in the 1980s.[16]

Recollections on the Strasshof deportations are also specific from a gendered perspective. Outside of the capital, Budapest, it was the only case when entire families had a chance to survive and therefore the recollections are by both men and women. However, in the case of Strasshof, the narrative of men of working age is almost entirely missing. The experience of the deportations from the Hungarian provinces in 1944 is conveyed by overtly female narratives. This was due to the fact that the bulk of the young adult Jewish men able to work, the labour servicemen, were ultimately spared the deportation. With rare exceptions, only boys under sixteen and men over fifty years old remained in the ghettos and were later deported. Few of them survived the concentration camps, and therefore most of the testimonies, memoirs and other first-hand accounts covering this chapter of the Holocaust were produced by women. Labour service, by contrast, was almost exclusively a male narrative, even though at the very end of the war thousands of women also shared this fate.

The first and primary goal of the Nazis following the invasion of Hungary was to obtain 100,000 Jewish "workers," notwithstanding their genocidal aims. Unexpectedly, very soon after the occupation, Adolf Eichmann reached an agreement with the over-zealous pro-Nazi collaborationists of the Hungarian government about a

---

16 Braham 1981, 1994 and 2016, Szita 1989 and 1991, Molnár 1995 and 2000, Schiller 1996, Bauer 1996, Lappin-Eppel et al. 2006, Suchy 2011, Frojimovics and Kovács 2015.

comprehensive deportation. As a result, Hungarian state administration deported all Jews living in the provinces, except the labour servicemen, simply because the Hungarian army was unwilling to hand them over. They even issued further summonses to call up as many Jewish men for labour service as possible. It is ironic that labour service, formulated in a rabidly antisemitic context, ultimately became an avenue of rescue. Historians often refer to this decision as a "rescue operation" to thwart Nazi genocidal plans. The situation was actually more complex, similar to the case of the Strasshof deportations. The series of events that ultimately saved the lives of labour servicemen were the results of conflicting antisemitic policies and a rivalry between and within various levels of power structure. The army followed its own antisemitic agenda and was unwilling to hand over a valuable workforce. In fact, deportation of the labour servicemen was only suspended.

The same interpretation applies to the decisions of head of state Regent Miklós Horthy, who first gave his consent to the deportations of the Jews from the provinces but then "saved" the Jews of Budapest in the summer of 1944, motivated mostly by pragmatic considerations. Just as in other Nazi satellite states, Jews remained the pawns in the endgame; that is, there was no ultimate decision about their fate, and sacrificing them for the war effort or political gain had remained an option until their countries broke with the Axis alliance or were defeated.

The fate of László Frenkel and his 15,000 fellow prisoners who arrived in Strasshof at the end of June 1944 can also be understood in this interpretative framework. In László's words, the deportees were "hostages," kept alive for rational reasons, and danger was looming over them until the very end. Granted, they were in a somewhat privileged position compared to most Jewish prisoners trapped in the Nazi camp "archipelago," regarded as a potential reserve for further negotiations.

Nazi ideology had enjoyed mass support in Austria; however, by 1944, many Austrians had tired of the war and turned against Nazi policy. Of course, many did so in the knowledge of looming defeat. Therefore, local citizens, out of pragmatic or humanistic considerations, often treated the Jewish prisoners well, showed sympathy or even offered aid, and local authorities were often lenient in their treatment of Jews.

Another key aspect of survival in Strasshof was that the deported families were kept together. Although taking care of grandparents, invalids and small children could involve extra tasks and a source of worries, it also provided other family members with invaluable emotional support and a sense of belonging. In the family camps, the elderly could actually offer practical support: they took care of the children and cooked if facilities were available. However, the elderly or sick who stayed behind from work got a much smaller ration of food, so it was in the families' vital interest to send every capable member, often even children under twelve, to work.

Leslie Fazekas's memoir and diary, *In Dreams Together*, provides us with an exceptional perspective on the Strasshof deportations. He had been spared from labour service until 1944. Then, he was drafted for service and was among the few labour servicemen who were eventually deported, due to specific circumstances, along with his family. The people around him who had been forced into the cattle car were almost exclusively women, children, the sick and the elderly. László, on the verge of adulthood, had to become the *de facto* head of the family all of a sudden, and he was able to rely on his mental and physical strength, self-confidence and nearly endless optimism.

On July 1, 1944, the day the transport arrived in Strasshof, Judit and László were forcibly separated, although the couple did not completely lose contact while in the labour camps. The Frenkel family was taken to District XI of Vienna (Simmering), where nearly 1,500 prisoners of various nationalities performed slave labour for Österreichische Saurerwerke AG, a war production plant under the administration of the Mauthausen camp complex. Saurerwerke, originally an automobile factory, mostly produced tanks, armoured vehicles and military trucks during the war. The cohort of Hungarian Jews working there included thirty men, sixty-four women and seventeen children. Only 51 of the 111 prisoners were able to work. They lived in a small family camp nearby.

László Frenkel's diary offers a detailed description of the living and working conditions in this camp, relatively bearable as compared to the conditions for the majority of Jewish deportees in and around Vienna.[17] The food supply was initially quite poor, but later improved significantly, and László did not face any problems in this respect until the last weeks of Nazi rule, when the food supply collapsed. However, the lack of adequate winter clothes and shoes, as well as the increasing air raids late in the war, posed a constant problem and danger for all prisoners.

Fifteen-year-old Judit Felbermann and her family were sent to the northern part of Vienna (District XXII, Aspern) where a group of forty-one prisoners, including eleven men, twenty-six women and four children (thirty-five were able to work), toiled in the fields of a local farmer, Hans Oberleuthner. Agricultural labour was not at all easier than working in the factory and also not without risks. Furthermore, as described in one of the few letters Judit managed to send to László, the Felbermanns lived in quite miserable conditions in Aspern. The prisoners were crammed together in a wooden barrack with a broken roof, which allowed the rain to fall in. People lay

---

17 A fellow prisoner of László's, fourteen-year-old Béla Varga, recalled that the *Meister* overseeing the factory work in the day shift, Ants Lachman, was "not a Nazi and was a true friend of the Jewish workers," and that the foremen on the night shift, Johann Winkler and Josef Lukawsky, "were also quite nice people." *Nehéz napok* [*Hard days*]. The diary of Béla Varga, Collections of the Holocaust Memorial Center, Budapest.

on sacks of straw on the bare cement floor and could not sleep during the night because of the rodents. There was no electricity or running water, and people had to use three small washbasins to clean. Due to improper clothing, footwear and blankets, they were freezing, and many got sick.[18]

With the winter approaching, farmers had no use for most of the agricultural workers. As a result, some 2, 200 Hungarian prisoners were deported to the Bergen-Belsen concentration camp, where many of them ultimately perished.[19] Judit's group, however, was spared this fate. They were taken to a camp maintained by the City of Vienna in Floridsdorf (District XXI), in a former school building. Those who could work cleared rubble and snow; others worked for the Shell company. The circumstances here, as described by Judit, were much worse than in Simmering, where László stayed.

Hungarian slave labourers in Vienna could rely on the remaining institutional network of the largely diminished local Jewish community. It is striking that in the sixth year of Nazi persecution, when so many local Jews had been murdered, certain parts of this network still functioned and offered invaluable support not only for the few thousand Jews still living in Vienna, but for Hungarian Jewish deportees as well. Leslie's diary and letters demonstrate that the hospital of the Viennese Jewish community, under head physician and director Dr. Emil Tuchmann, did everything to support the Hungarian prisoners. They performed serious, often life-saving operations, and offered regular treatment, such as dental and eye care for the slave

---

18 Report of physician Dr. Theodor Israel Friedländer to Dr. Emil Tuchmann, physician-director of the Jewish Hospital of Vienna and member of the Jewish Council, 4 September 1944. The Archive of the Vienna Wiesenthal Institute for Holocaust Studies, Records of the People's Court of Vienna, File No. 770/1946.

19 Eleonore Lappin-Eppel, "Deportations of Hungarian Jews to Austria (1944/45)" in *Jewish Studies at the CEU, Vol. VII, 2009–2011,* András Kovács and Michael Miller, eds., 63-82.

labourers, which was a unique feature in the Nazi camp system. The hospital also had a key role in creating a communication network for the prisoners: László and Judit could exchange letters mostly due to the selfless help of the hospital staff.[20]

Some cultural and religious activities were permitted in the camps and prisoners often could move relatively freely in the city. Judit managed to get permission to leave the camp along with her mother and visit László four times between early February and early March. They could use public transportation until the middle of March, when the bombings destroyed the streetcar wires.

With the front line approaching, German authorities started to evacuate the surviving prisoners to the Mauthausen concentration camp system, mostly on foot marches, as transport facilities were no longer available. Many Hungarian Jewish prisoners perished from hunger and diseases, froze to death or fell victim to retreating SS troops who took vicious revenge on defenceless people.[21]

László and Judit, although still apart, were ultimately spared from further mass deportations and death marches. They were liberated in Vienna by Red Army troops, who captured the city on April 13, 1945.

László's diary entries not only meticulously detail everyday life, social relations, living and working conditions in the labour camp, but they also provide the reader with insights into internal relations and conflicts, as well as the survival strategies of the prisoners. He

---

20 Kinga Frojimovics and Éva Kovács, "Jews in a 'Judenrein' City: Hungarian Jewish Slave Laborers in Vienna (1944–1945)" in *Hungarian Historical Review*, Vol. 4. No. 3 (2015), 705–736.

21 On the night of May 2 to 3, 1945, unidentified SS soldiers shot dead 228 Hungarian Jews, mostly women and children, at Hofamt Priel (Persenbeug), including some of László Frenkel's former fellow prisoners. On the Hofamt Priel massacre and other war crimes committed against Jewish forced labourers, see Eleonore Lappin-Eppel, *Ungarisch-jüdische Zwangsarbeiterinnen und Zwangsarbeiter in Österreich, 1944/45* (Vienna-Berlin: Lit, 2010), 174–193.

maintained a positive approach to hardships (as much as possible) throughout, a form of inner resistance. His main concern was the welfare of his parents and other family members. He cared for them relentlessly and compassionately, in a self-sacrificing manner. He seemingly suffered the most from boredom, and he took comfort in counting the days and calculating the possibility of seeing his Judit again. As if love had cast a spell upon both of them, they never doubted that their significant other would survive and that they would be reunited after the madness ended. In actuality, death was close: in the form of continuous air raids, accidents, illnesses and privation, and even at the very end, in the form of death marches and arbitrary killings. However, László and Judit survived, due to their exceptional endurance and mere luck. They got married after the war and ultimately made the fairy-tale cliché "lived happily ever after" come true. Their wartime letters and Leslie's postwar memoir are not only precious sources of historical research, but also stand as a persuasive testament of love, loyalty and human resilience.

László Csősz
Historian and senior archivist, National Archives of Hungary
Claims Conference University Partnership in Holocaust Studies
Lecturer, ELTE University
2020

Dr. Csősz's research was supported by a fellowship at the Wiener Holocaust Library, the EHRI Fellowship at the Vienna Wiesenthal Institute for Holocaust Studies and the project at the Institute of Contemporary History, Czech Academy of Sciences, funded by the Grant Agency of the Czech Republic.

Editorial Note

While in captivity as a forced labourer in Austria during World War II, Leslie Fazekas (then László Frenkel, also referred to as Laci) wrote a diary in Hungarian from August 1944 to April 1945. He addressed almost all of his diary entries to his girlfriend, Judit Felbermann (also known as Judith, or Judy, Felberman), whom he was separated from. By September 1944, Leslie and Judy had found a way to write letters and postcards to each other. Leslie was able to hold onto his diary throughout the war years and after, and when he and Judy reunited, and later married, they held dear all the letters they had been able to keep as well.

In preparing Leslie Fazekas's extraordinary diary, letters and memoir for publication, a number of decisions were made by the editor of this volume, Arielle Berger, in consultation with the author, Leslie Fazekas, and the scholar and introduction writer who annotated and advised on this book, László Csősz.

In the section that follows, "Diary and Letters August 1944–April 1945," the diary and letters are presented in sequence as much as possible — that is, in the sequence the letters were written, not necessarily when they were postmarked or received — for the reader to better understand the chronology of events and communication. Letters have been presented in italics to differentiate them from the diary entries, presented in roman type. Paragraphs have been generated for

easier reading of lengthy diary entries and letters, editorial clarifica-
tions and definitions have been inserted in square brackets, and footnotes have been added to help the reader understand certain details
in the text.

The translators were able to work off the original, preserved 1944
letters, as well as the original diary entries for most of the dates in
October 1944, and all subsequent entries up until the end of the diary in April 1945. For the 1944 diary entries from August to October,
the translators needed to rely on a postwar typewritten version in
Hungarian, as the original diary entries from those dates were lost
at some point over the course of the interceding years. Additional-
ly, the author had also translated the full spectrum of his own diary
and letters at some point in the 1990s, so this provided a rich source
for comparison and clarification of events and expressions and also
helped to fill in two entries that could not be recovered.

In Dreams Together has been prepared with great effort and a detailed diligence to the original text. Leslie's diary is replete with references to poets, writers and playwrights, showing that, as a teenager
whose education was disrupted by the war, learning was still of the
utmost importance to him. The author's postwar memoir, partially
written from thousands of pages of writing Leslie continued to record in a diary after 1955, is equally an invaluable source for learning
about Leslie's pre-war childhood and young adulthood, the love that
shaped his life, and his reflections, as an adult, on how he survived
the Holocaust.

Maps

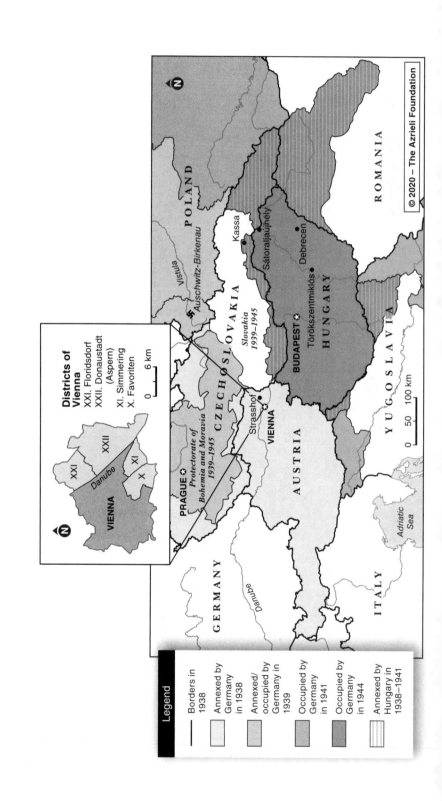

Legend

— Borders in 1938

Annexed by Germany in 1938

Annexed/occupied by Germany in 1939

Occupied by Germany in 1941

Occupied by Germany in 1944

Annexed by Hungary in 1938–1941

Districts of Vienna

XXI. Floridsdorf
XXII. Donaustadt (Aspern)
XI. Simmering
X. Favoriten

0   6 km

© 2020 – The Azrieli Foundation

GERMANY

POLAND

Vistula

Auschwitz-Birkenau

Danube

PRAGUE ✪
Protectorate of Bohemia and Moravia
1939–1945

CZECHOSLOVAKIA

SLOVAKIA
Slovakia
1939–1945

Kassa

Sátoraljaújhely

Debrecen

Törökszentmiklós

BUDAPEST ☆

HUNGARY

ROMANIA

Strasshof

VIENNA

AUSTRIA

ITALY

Adriatic Sea

YUGOSLAVIA

0   50   100 km

DEBRECEN, 1944

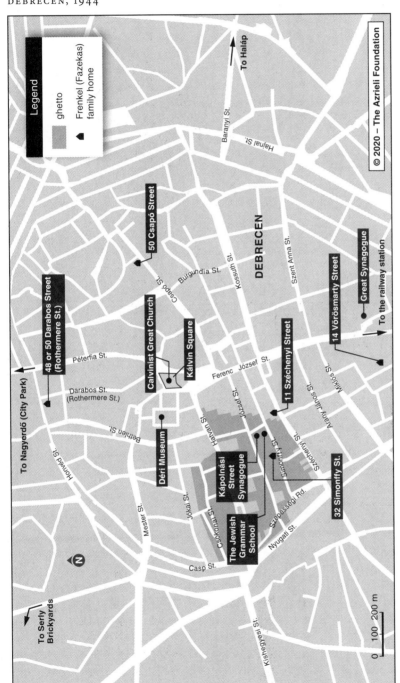

Legend

ghetto

Frenkel (Fazekas) family home

© 2020 – The Azrieli Foundation

DEBRECEN

50 Csapó Street

Great Synagogue

To the railway station

14 Vörösmarty Street

48 or 50 Darabos Street (Rothermere St.)

Calvinist Great Church

Kálvin Square

11 Széchenyi Street

Darabos St. (Rothermere St.)

Déri Museum

Kápolnási Street Synagogue

The Jewish Grammar School

32 Simonffy St.

To Nagyerdő (City Park)

To Serly Brickyards

To Haláp

Baranyi St.

Hajnal St.

Burgundia St.

Kossuth St.

Szent Anna St.

Péterfia St.

Csapó St.

Ferenc József St.

Bethlen St.

Hatvan St.

József St.

Simonffy St.

Miklós St.

Arany János St.

Széchenyi St.

Honvéd St.

Mester St.

Jókai St.

Csokonai St.

Szepességi Rd.

Nyugati St.

Casp St.

Kishegyesi St.

0 100 200 m

N

Diary and Letters

A page from Leslie's diary, December 1944.

Thursday, August 10, 1944 at 16:00 [4:00 p.m.]
My dear Judit,

I'm not at all surprised that Kelemen Mikes[1] spent his time in captivity writing letters to an imaginary aunt. At least that way you can converse to your heart's content. However, Mikes at least had friends during his captivity with whom he could discuss current events and their projections, or impressions, into his inner world. But I am, as Babits would put it, a blue, brooding, broken-down, buddyless bloke, a blundering boob.[2] Or, without the alliteration, someone without a friend or a kindred spirit to speak to for a month and a half now.

---

1 Kelemen Mikes (1690–1761) was a confidant of Ferenc Rákóczy, leader of an anti-Habsburg Hungarian uprising, who settled in Turkey after the defeat of his cause in 1711. Mikes's *Letters from Turkey* documented the everyday life of the Hungarian political refugees. The fictitious letters were addressed to his non-existent aunt.

2 Paraphrasing the alliterative poem "Far far away" by the Hungarian poet Mihály Babits (1883–1941). Entry translated by Marietta Morry and Lynda Muir.

August 11 at 16:00 [4:00 p.m.]

I could not continue yesterday, so I am now picking up where I left off. For the past three weeks, you have been the only thought in my mind. Where can you be? How is life treating you? (Not for a moment did I fear that you might no longer be alive; I am certain that you are.) How do you feel without me? I couldn't get these thoughts out of my mind, and my favourite pastime has been looking at pictures of you. On the whole, though, my mood has been decent. I found comfort in the thought that being separated had a benefit in us not having to deal with bickering relatives on either side, and that such a long time without each other will reveal how indispensable you are to me, and will strengthen the bond between us further. (I always consider Saturday, July 1, as the day my misfortunes began, because that is when we parted.[3] In hindsight everything seems to have been just fine up to that point, even the cattle car.)

This is how things went until the middle of the week. Then a few people here went to the hospital and they came back telling us how well the Jews were treated at other locations [camps]. Since then, I've been troubled night and day. All I can think of is that I am being punished for having left you. If I had waited for you, I am sure I would have ended up in a better place myself.[4]

I have only four hours of peace each day, when I sleep from 8:00 [a.m.] to 12:00 [p.m.] in the morning, as if I'd been knocked on the head. At night in the factory I picture you constantly, longing to be with you; I would forget all my troubles, the poor food and all. In this

---

3 The date the transport from Debrecen, Hungary, arrived in Strasshof, Austria. On subsequent pages the date is mentioned as Sunday, July 2.

4 Living and working conditions, as well as treatment of forced labourers, differed from camp to camp. However, prisoners were not in the position to make decisions about what camps and work sites they were assigned to.

state I yearn for freedom not once, but a million times more desperately than if you were by my side. There is this girl at the factory, the *Meister's* [master's] girlfriend, who reminds me of you a lot. The very sight of her each night fills my eyes with tears. "Oh, if you were here, I would be the Meister!" I can no longer bear it without freedom. Everything seems to have conspired against me. It's not only that we don't have any freedom, but our work is the most awful night shift, from 7:30 [p.m.] to 6:30 [a.m.] six nights a week, and the food we get is terrible, and the portions are not enough to survive on.

If only I could get to the place where you are (if I knew at all where that place is) that would mean life itself to me. As it is, I am a dead man, dead in the intellectual sense, because I am unable to continue my studies as my nerves are being eroded by having to work all night long, and dead in spirit, focused as I am on the single obsession of longing to see you again.

See, I am feeling better now that I have vented all these complaints, and I believe I will be able to show you this letter one day, and that's something at least. Just love me the way I love you! I never told you anything like this before, nor did I ask you to be faithful to me when we said goodbye, because I was convinced that you were mine and would belong to me forever. But have you read "Two Prisoners?"[5]

I conclude this letter in the hope that this past week has been the darkest one, and the others will be rosier. I am determined to continue this diary-like correspondence (à la Mikes) so that we may read it together some time, some place, with smiles on our faces. Many kisses until we see each other again.

---

5 *Két fogoly* (1926) was a popular novel by Lajos Zilahy, a well-known Hungarian writer in the 1930s. The story is about a young couple separated by World War I. The young man is taken to a prisoner-of-war camp, believed to be dead, and the girl marries another man.

Sunday, August 13, at 17:00 [5:00 p.m.]
My dear Judit,

It is now clear to me that I am going to write a diary instead of let-ters, as I did back at home, if not every single day for lack of time. Yet addressing these entries to you, and even this explanation, makes it seem like writing letters. Putting your name at the top of each entry indicates that I think of you every passing day, every minute of my life here. The last time I wrote, two days ago, I was in a lousy mood. By yesterday my spirit had lightened up, and I even sang songs at work at night, until my throat was raw. I am all too aware, though, that this cheerfulness is artificial, like back in the brickyard, when I sensed a dark future looming large even as I laughed all day long. Here, too, I kept laughing and was in good spirits (empty good spirits!), trying not to think too much, but at least I wasn't feeling as despondent as before.

I have just come back from the bathroom, bringing a glass of wa-ter for my father. He says that the Jews of Pest are still there, but that does not make me bitter.[6] All is well that ends well. Someday this whole thing will be nothing but a memory.

I did some studying in the morning and in the afternoon today, as I had before last week, chewing on *Wiener cakes* [bread crusts]. I got a little tired of all that study, so I am returning to the diary. But for the noise around me caused by these girls! I am thinking about how it would be if Judit and I, just the two of us, went some place else where I could tell her all in peace…. But all that is futile, because I am here, alive and laughing! It doesn't matter that fate put me here, in this situation. I'm not sorry, and I have no regrets. After all, every place is what you make of it.

---

6 Leslie means that the Jews of Budapest have not been deported. See the introduc-tion for more information.

Today I was upset during lunch time, but I have only myself to blame for it. This reminds me to note that the reason I felt so miserable last time was because *dörrgemüse*[7] was announced for dinner. Now I feel more optimistic, as we are told that the food will improve. In fact, yesterday (for the first time in six weeks) we had pear supplement with our porridge for dinner, no less! Today it's jam, curd cheese and rice with sauce.

Monday, August 14, 1944 at 8:00 a.m.
My dear Judit,

As I was writing down the last words of my diary entry yesterday, they yelled, "Dinner's here," and I left it all and rushed to get a plate. I ate all of the curd cheese but saved the jam for the night shift, as that will keep. It is morning now, so not much could have happened since last night. I only wanted to say that I believe in being freed from here more strongly than ever before…. I can hardly wait until November 1, to find out what will happen then and until that date.[8]

As we recited poetry last night, I was shocked to find that there was not a single poem I knew entirely by heart. I haven't been studying since March [1944] and have forgotten a lot. Trains of thought no longer crisscross my mind, but frankly, I learn anything mathematical just as easily as I used to, so this latest hiatus of seven months, from March to November,[9] will not cause a setback I can't handle. Then I'll get down to studying in earnest. It's all right. Mom reminds me that last week I told her she would have to mop the floor six more times. I

---

7 A dish made of dried vegetables (German).
8 Leslie and Judit had agreed to try and meet back in Debrecen on the first day of every other month, if at all possible, were they to be separated in Austria.
9 In 1944, the school year had ended in April due to the events of war, for both Jews and non-Jews. Mentioning the month of November here reveals his hope that the war would end by that date.

am telling her she now has only five times left. I want to celebrate my birthday at home because of a bet I made with Lili Nasch yesterday. I claimed there were still Jews in Budapest, which she denies. In any case, we will change the stakes to two litres of liqueur and a bottle of champagne, which we will drink on my birthday, September 28. I am lying in bed now. I'm going to have a slice of bread with jam, and then I'll sleep until noon.

Tuesday, August 15, 1944 at 17:00 [5:00 p.m.]
My dear Judit,

I am now quite content with my circumstances. After all, work is not hard at the factory (the machine is automatic[10]), I slowly got used to staying up at night, and the food is not all that bad really — today we had peas with sausage and even some sweet yeast bread to supplement the ration of bread we get. If it goes on like this, we will not starve to death! Feldheim has just returned from the hospital. He says there are places much worse than this, and we should be happy to be here. And he is right. As far as I am concerned, I am happy to be here (except that I wish Judit was here with me, rather than I there with her). But I will be strong and study a lot. In fact I have studied today already even though it's a weekday. I will put in another hour tomorrow, and I may review my calculus by the time we get back here, at the very least. As for the news…what news? I will make notes on Freud and my readings in biology, and even compile synopses of certain topics if I have the time and enough paper.

Saturday, August 19, 1944 at 16:00 [4:00 p.m.]
My dear Judit,

---

10 The machine was actually semi-automatic, see the diary entry of October 11, 1944.

September 1, the day I have been waiting for, will be here soon. How long have I been hoping that it will fall on a magnificent day like this! I will be waiting for you in the late summer sun. You will rush to me joyously, and we shall never part again. I have pictured this scenario so many times. The picture includes the post office and the Déri Museum, where we will go out for a walk, checking out the old places and the benches, many of which still have my name carved in the wood. Then perhaps we will go to the baths outside the city, and I will perhaps get the same strange feeling I always get when I come back after a long time away from home. But this picture is slowly fading away. The summer sun yields to a wet autumn day as I stand shivering in my winter coat, turning up my collar, staring at the gloomy patter of the rain. I am waiting for you. I will be standing there motionless, perhaps for hours, waiting anxiously, with my heart racing. Are you still coming, or is it that I will never see you again after that day on July 1 when we so cheerfully waved goodbye? (Remember what I told you then? I said we would meet again the next day. Since then fifty days, seven weeks have passed.) So I am standing there with my heart pounding, and then all of a sudden you appear, just as fresh and lovely as when we parted. Because that's how I liked you most, when you had lost that bit of weight. Our reunion will be a happy one, beyond words. So happy that I can't even imagine it as I sit by this table in our barrack. I am only praying that the sullen drizzle never turns into muddy, black slush. And that I may see you again in this life!

Unwittingly, this diary entry has assumed the shape of a letter so far, so let me now get back to writing to myself, which is a mode of writing more objective and more subjective at the same time.... If this past week was any good for me at all, it was because I had the opportunity to witness two loves, two love stories, from close by: the wild, romantic love of a young girl, and the impassioned, blazing love of an Italian youth. He is the quintessential Italian lover, for whom the only thing that matters is to love and be loved in return, even at the risk of being imprisoned or shot to death.

Monday, August 21, 1944 at 14:00 [2:00 p.m.]
My dear Judit,

I am lying here behind the barracks (in the spot marked xx).[11] The picture you see is that of our barrack, with the fence, and our room is the one in the rear on the left, overlooking the doctor's place. I am now between the barrack and the [air-raid] shelter. I came here after lunch to get some sleep, but I can't, so I am going to write for a while. It is becoming difficult, unfortunately, because nothing is happening here. We are simply vegetating. I spend six days a week at the factory, standing by the machine from 19:30 [7:30 p.m.] to 6:30 [a.m.], so even thinking meaningful thoughts is out of the question. (I tried when I felt very drowsy, but I couldn't.) Then we get back, sleep from 8:00 to 12:00, have lunch until 1:00 or 1:30, then sleep again or, what's worse, just toss and turn in our beds until 6:00. Then we clean up, have dinner until 6:45, then linger outside in the courtyard until 7:00, waiting for the *Werkschutz* [factory security]. Then it starts all over again.

This is our daily schedule from Monday night to Sunday morning. This is followed by more sleeping time, then lunch till 1:30, and then, we finally get Sunday afternoon off. We usually sit in the courtyard talking until 9:00.[12] Monday morning and afternoon are spent sleeping, and in the evening it's back to the factory again. Let me add that, with this way of life, time passes rather quickly, and next thing you know, a week has gone by. We sleep through the day, and the nights are often over before you know it.

There was a time when I used to think that the more meaningfully

---

11 It is likely that a drawing was attached to the original.

12 Leslie relayed that the talk was sometimes about the time when they were free, but that mainly people conversed about how to cook certain dishes and how they tasted. This was a common topic of conversation among prisoners in many Nazi camps.

you spend your time the more slowly it will pass. But a day teeming with events will last just as long as a week just as busy. Just think about how much can happen from morning till night! Our entire stay here, now into week seven, has been so empty that it's not worth a single day. I have had only two experiences that enriched me, and even these two are fused in my memory. One is the recognition that I am still young but have already learned what it means to live for the past. (My future is so obscure that it seems futile to make advance calculations.) The other is the love I have now is nothing like I have felt before. The two fuse in the person of Judit. Whenever I ponder the past, I always end up with the theme of love. Does this girl really deserve all the love and thoughts that I expend on her? Gradually, though, both of these great themes cease to be directly related to my emotions. Now I am only concerned with the present, with taking care of myself, and am only using the past in order to draw strength from it. I hope the time will come when it will be realistic to think of the future.

August 26, 1944 at 17:00 [5:00 p.m.]
My dear Judit,

I have sad news to record today. Last night Mom discovered a tumour in her breast. She waited until the morning when we came back from the factory to tell us. She says she didn't sleep all night, just stayed awake crying. She thought it was malignant and that she would never see us again. She told us all this in tears this morning. She had the tumour checked by the physician, who said she should be tested at the Jewish hospital. We will need to wait for a doctor from Vienna to issue the referral. We are all very worried and can already feel how much we will miss her when she is in hospital.

I used to think it would have made no difference if I had ended up in a labour camp in Hungary by myself, without them [my family]. Now I understand that it would have been hell, especially if I didn't hear from them. Being here, I can be a bit more confident about Mom as well. Even if it does turn out to be cancer, God forbid, it cannot be all that bad, because it's been caught at an early stage. I am sure we will see each other again soon. And being away from us will be terrible for Mom, too. I know that is why she is crying all the time; it is not for herself. Who is going to say good morning to me when I return from the night shift? Who is going to kiss me goodbye as I leave in the evening? It's going to be Mom's memory, no one else. And the faith that she will soon be back, healthier and stronger than before. This hope will make waiting for her easier to bear.

Just when things begin to look up, something must always happen! A while ago we petitioned for getting some food during the night, and finally it seems we will get something to eat on the shift starting next Monday — bread for sure, and possibly something else, too. So everything seemed to be working out well, and then this crash comes out of the blue, changing our lives here completely. From now on the three of us [Leslie, his brother and their father] will have to look after ourselves. It is a sorry state to be in. Now Mom is going to be hospitalized for some time, maybe for a month, and we may not even hear about her all this time, while bombing raids and world-changing events may happen, and we will be kept apart from her. But we will have to find a way to see her, just as I must find a way to see Judit, because this is my family, this is all I need and nothing else. Now it's a time without Judit, without Mother, without books. Only faith to go by. And how much strength we can draw from the faintest ray of hope! But I have no time left to continue this reflection, thank God. I must be getting ready for the night shift at the factory.

Thursday, August 31, 1944 at 13:00 [1:00 p.m.]
My dear Judit,

The day of our first designated date has arrived, and I feel so weak and ill that I would be unable to attend our rendezvous even if I were free.

Yesterday I got very sick with an upset stomach (and an intestinal infection) from the cantaloupe we had Saturday evening. I haven't had a bite to eat since then, and I look like a skeleton. Yesterday the disease peaked with a fever of 39 °C. My temperature is back to normal now but I can't stand up straight for more than five minutes, weakened as I am by six days of fasting. My mood has improved to the point that I am now confident I will be able to keep our next appointment. As you know, one's mood is always determined by external circumstances. Well, the food here is getting better. Next week, when I go back to work, we will get *zubusz*[13] even at the factory. I will have missed three days of work (yesterday, today and tomorrow) due to my sickness, which is not much. I will survive, but I feel exhausted now. I am going to continue later.

Friday, September 1, 1944 at 17:00 [5:00 p.m.]
My dear Judit and Mother,

I am feeling well enough to pick up my shift at the factory tonight. Now it's a different trouble, a different anxiety. Mom went to the hospital after 7:00 in the morning and has not returned. I wonder if she will be released today or kept in for surgery. The others who went in with her will tell us what's happening. All afternoon we have been listening carefully for the car to arrive, ready to meet her when she comes — but all in vain.

Saturday, September 9, 1944 at 16:00 [4:00 p.m.]
My dear Judit,

It's been a long time since I last wrote anything. Meanwhile, that famous date of ours came and went, leaving nothing but painful

---

13 *Zubuße* (German): supplement, an extra portion of food.

thoughts. Mom's tumour has turned out to be benign, thank God, but she feels very sick and feeble after the surgery, so she must be attended to all day long. This is one reason I do not even have five minutes to write. Not that I have anything to say, given that I hate writing down the same things twice. The only thing worthy of mention is the recent improvement in the quality of the food we get. The Russians[14] have also been given equal status with the Germans, so they too get much better food now: meat three times a week, things like soup, potatoes with onion sauce. We have potatoes in some form three times a week; it was potatoes in tomato sauce for dinner last night. In this way not only have I stopped losing weight but have begun to pack on kilos, obviously due to the dinner supplement we get two or three times a week. This in addition to the slab of margarine, the jar of jam and the three loaves of bread that I have saved for needy days, so we have enough food to be eating all day if we wanted to. If only Mom would feel better! She is sadly emaciated and is still unable to take food.

Our next appointment date is my birthday, September 28 (Judit's is around this time, too). I wonder how many things will happen up to then. We have had a visit by a woman from Vienna.[15] I wrote down Judit's name on a slip of paper, asking the lady to find out her whereabouts. We shall see. And now let's get some cooking done!

Wednesday, September 20, 1944 at 16:00 [4:00 p.m.]
My dear Judit,

I am having another sleepless night. I haven't had a book with me for three months, and I can't just stare at the ceiling forever. At times like

---

14 Soviet prisoners of war.

15 The visitor was a representative of the Red Cross, as clarified by Leslie in his memoir.

this, I always end up eating, and I don't feel like doing it again. It's been a while since I last wrote, so I have enough to write about now, even in this generally uneventful mood.

First of all, I make a note for the record that the day before yesterday, the woman from Vienna who comes by every Monday told me you all were in Aspern [District x x i i of Vienna], near that large airport. At least now my thoughts have a geographical direction whenever I think of you. (Even though you have no idea where I am.) So this was the big event for Monday, in addition to it being the start of the New Year.[16] Sunday night we were all moved as the New Year drew close. Women and even men were crying, not for their sins but perhaps for the year we left behind. Someone wished the nights passed as fast as our weeks are going by, one after the next. It is hard to believe that, for the nearly two weeks since I last wrote, the only thing that has really happened with me was this nasty indigestion, from which I have recovered so well that I am thinking about food all the time. And that Pista at the factory fabricated a chess set we can play with. Seen in this light, all this time is hardly worth a day's events. True enough, if you can call it an event, I have come to tolerate staying up at night very well, despite the fact that I only get some sleep in the morning hours. Not that this has helped to advance my studies in any way. I have been ignoring my mathematics, as a discipline where only constant, uninterrupted study is worth anything. It's only once in a while that I pick up my exercise book, to check if I have grown too dumb and ignorant. (Yes, I have.)

Now we are using up the remaining supplies we brought along from home. What comes next we do not really know. We are not even going to get the *zubusz*[17] at the factory from now on. We badly need to stash away some bread, but we don't have any!

---

16 Rosh Hashanah, the Jewish New Year. See the glossary for information on this holiday.
17 See the footnote related to the diary entry of August 31.

Wien, 25.09.1944
To: Mr. László Frenkel
[stamped on back] Hans Oberleuthner
Landwirt
Wien xxii/148, Ehrensteing. 9
Tel. f -22-2-37

Dear Gazsi,[18]

I am finally able to send you a note via someone I have found. I have tried several times before; I hope this time it will work. We are working in Aspern, District xxii. My address is: J.F. Wien xxii. 148 c/o Hans Oberleuthner, Ehrenstein Gasse 9. Write as much and as often as you can. Imre [Steuer] and his family are with us, as is Uncle Jancsi. Let me know if you find out anything about Miklós Fülöp. I got here [to the hospital] when I broke my eyeglasses on the job threshing wheat and had to come in to the hospital to have a new pair made. But now I am out of paper. Greetings to everyone, and you especially,
    Judith
    I will send you a postcard as well.

Tuesday, September 26, 1944 at 16:00 [4:00 p.m.]
My dear Judit,

The second date on which we were planning to meet is coming soon. It's my birthday on Wednesday. I have always been proud of having been born on Yom Kippur day, according to the Jewish calendar, on the night that every Jew spends fasting. This year is the first since I

---

18 A nickname that Judit called Leslie. An image of this letter is on page 146.

was born when Yom Kippur falls on September 27, perhaps signalling that this birthday will be a milestone as important as that first one.[19] But superstitions aside, I am certain that we are going to see a quick succession of remarkable dates. The first three months here may have been sluggish, but the months from now on will rush past rapidly. My birthday will be soon followed by November 1, then Christmas and January 1.

Autumn has descended on the barracks, and we are getting ready for what we expect will be a harsh winter. We are now asking the woman from Vienna for warm clothes rather than food. Life here is becoming more cozy. Now I have a German dictionary at hand, so I can go on learning German. I plan on memorizing 800 German words a month, well enough to use them if need be. I have become better at organizing my day and economizing on the bread, and have learned how to get some sleep in the afternoon. So everything is quite all right, except that I think we will have to yield our room to the kids when the weather turns cold. Thank God, Mom has recovered completely and is now eating well. (I only think about eating, though.)

My dear Judit, I have been thinking of you a great deal again lately. The dates of our planned meetings come and go swiftly, but every one of them leaves a deep imprint on my soul. Time gradually becomes meaningless, and months no longer have any significance. My soul will be like a clean slate, ready to receive new impressions. The present is like farmland that lies fallow. In the future my soul will become more fertile. And that's when I will truly be able to love you.

---

9 In 1925, Leslie was born on erev Yom Kippur, September 27; however, in the official birth register, his birthday was recorded as September 28. In 1944, Yom Kippur began on September 26 and concluded on September 27. Here, Leslie is referring to his actual day of birth as September 27; elsewhere, he notes that his birthday is September 28.

Monday, October 2, 1944 at 15:00 [3:00 p.m.]
My dear Judit,

Today I need to write, if for no other reason than that it is another notable day: It is precisely a quarter of a year ago that we arrived here in this Lager, and a quarter-year since I last saw you, my Judit! Little did we know that on that Saturday when we said goodbye, in the assurance that we would meet the next day! A quarter-year is a long time under normal circumstances, filled with struggle and endeavour. By contrast, I can safely say that this past quarter-year has been one of the most carefree periods of my life, but also one of the dullest, dreariest and most boring. This is why this long stretch of time went by so fast. Time here only seems long during the moment it is passing, but these days will not add much of anything to our past, at best one-tenth of what such a respectably long period should deserve.[20]

As I am mainly inspired by this anniversary, I would have written anyway, and I will tell you why. I think about two days after we had arrived here, we were assigned a little room all to ourselves, separated from the rest of the barrack. The kids spent all day outside in the yard so as not to disturb the workers resting after their night shift. Yet cold weather comes to Vienna sooner than to Debrecen. As I am writing these lines, it is raining and chilly outside. I have a nasty cough because it is so cold at the factory that I freeze to the bone after just two hours, even though I wear a shirt, shorts over underpants, a sweater, a sweatshirt, a scarf and a spring overcoat. (I gave my winter coat to Father.) The weather having turned cold, the children can no longer spend all day outside, so we had to yield our room to them and move to the large barrack again. I cannot begin to describe what this means to us. In our own room we lived in total privacy, without interference

---

20 Leslie is paraphrasing Thomas Mann's novel *Der Zauberberg* (*The Magic Mountain*), published in 1924.

by anyone. We had no one quarrel with us, stare at our plates, nosing about what we were eating or doing. We had our stove to cook meals on (one was brought to the barrack a week ago) and so on and so forth. We lived in lavish comfort. Now the only comfort I can find is in my reminiscences.

Back at home we used to live surrounded by superb conveniences. I wouldn't have traded our flat for any other. In Haláp, the five of us had a splendid room, complete with cleaning and washing-up facilities. In the ghetto, Imre's fine room was my second home, but our own accommodations were not too bad either. In the brickyard, we had the best living quarters in every way. It was an agreeable place without crowded conditions, and we did not even have to work. People would come to visit me whenever they needed some relaxing peace and quiet.[21] Even in the cattle car I had the best nook of all, and then finally we had this separate room here in the barrack. I have been so spoiled that, after this move, I cannot imagine how we can live in such dire circumstances for any length of time.

There are some Italians now among us [...][22] Apparently, suffering so badly from homesickness is a condition unique to Hungarians, perhaps only the Jews. But I would say it's Hungarians. As the French say, you Hungarians do nothing but sit at home and eat all the time, like animals. The sons and daughters of other nations go around the whole world, but Hungarians will never trade their good food for knowledge and experience. They may be right, and if I could grow in knowledge and experience here, I would have no complaint. But the fact is that I have had less and less opportunity to do that. When I am

---

21 See Leslie's memoir for more on forced labour in Haláp, the Debrecen ghetto and the transit camp.

22 A reference to Italian prisoners of war. In the photocopy of the typewritten diary, the bottom of this page was cut off. Leslie had previously translated the continuation of this phrase with, "The Italian barber is here for my haircut. He says, nicht denken [do not think]."

free to choose, I will decide whether to return to Hungary right away or go out to the world to gain experience. As far as I can see it now, I'd rather vote for the latter option.

And now my last words are addressed to you, my Judit! Most people, regardless of their nationality, would sacrifice their lives for the one they love. In this I am no different from the rest. My longing for you will not diminish over time. The clearest proof of my love for you is that you are always on my mind, and nothing could make me happier than at least having someone to talk with about you. May good fortune stay by your side!

Wednesday, October 11, 1944 at 15:00 [3:00 p.m.]
My dear Judit,

This day is another memorable one, as I have finally received a letter from you [Judit's letter dated September 25]. I am going to record here a draft of the reply I am going to send you.[23]

I was very much surprised by your card, which I had not expected at all. You can imagine how elated I felt just to see a word written in your hand! Admittedly, though, I would have preferred to see a more relevant, more substantial letter from you. In fact, you do not say much apart from giving me your address. I wonder how you found out that I am here, or indeed if you know my address at all. What is the work you do? (Provide some details, beyond being assigned to the wheat-threshing team.) How is that job? Is it hard? How are your supervisors? Whom do you work with, and do you get along with them? How is the accommodation? What's the food like? What about your circumstances in general? How do you spend a typical day? etc… I would have expected all this information but you told

---

23 The letter that Leslie wrote to Judit is a replica of this diary entry and thus is not included.

me nothing apart from a bit of chit-chat, when I thought the deal was that we would tell each other about everything.

So let me be the one to begin. My address is Österr. Saurer Werke Wien xɪ/79, Haidequerstrasse 9. Lager 4 Wohnlager Baracke 39. So yes, we live in the barracks. Ours is equipped with all amenities, including a separate bathroom, washroom, a water closet, and we even had a room all to ourselves until recently. For more than a week now, four stoves have been providing heat in our barrack, which sleeps 120. In short, our accommodations are princely. The bad part is that I haven't met a single person I know and have virtually no one to share a word with all day. Even those of my own age have been assigned someplace else. Out of 120, only 50 of us (men aged 14 to 60 and women to 45) are required to work, so the majority consists of children and older people, both men and women.[24] The only boy is Sanyi Guttmann; the girls include Vera Pollák, the Nasch sisters, Klári Kovács, and that's it. Actually, even if I had worthy company, I would not find the time to talk with anyone, because we work at night, from 7:30 in the evening to 6:30 in the morning, six times a week. Luckily, the workload is very light. I am the one with the most difficult job description. This consists of attending to a machine by fastening a bolt, turning the machine on, and letting it run for 10 minutes at a time. This means I could sit down or catch some sleep in intervals, but I prefer to spend this time studying German, as I never feel sleepy on the job. That's strange, because I only really sleep well during the morning; in the afternoon I seldom sleep and then not much at that. Instead, I stay up writing and studying mathematics or German — both are useful ways of spending time.

Imre writes that he has heard our food is inferior. It was indeed bad for a while but has been improving lately. A few examples: Sunday:

---

[24] Leslie has clarified that there were one hundred and fourteen people in his barrack; this is also the number he writes in a later letter to Judit.

soup and potatoes with liver sauce for lunch; cheese, margarine and marmalade for dinner. Monday: soup, potatoes, mustard sauce for lunch; rice pudding for dinner (made from real rice and milk). Tuesday: soup, meat loaf with potatoes for lunch; creamy vegetables for dinner. Wednesday: soup and potatoes with tomato sauce for lunch; creamy vegetables, eggs, curd cheese and jam for dinner. Creamy vegetables on Friday and Saturday. And soup every day. [page partially cut off] …black coffee and one kilo of bread for three days. So the food is decent and almost sufficient.

I would love to go to the hospital just to meet you, but I am sound as a bell, so this leaves us with correspondence. If you or someone from your Lager goes to the hospital, leave a letter to me with Waltner (one of the patients) or József Auspitz (an attendant). They will find a way to forward it to me. I am going to do the same, so do seek them out. By the way, I wrote you a postcard a while back in Vienna. Did you receive it?

It's been 13 or 14 weeks since we last met, and all this time has flown by unnoticed. November 1 is approaching fast, but with God's help we won't need to honour our appointment as long as we can stay in touch in this way. Please write at least as much as I do, but only about what truly matters. We can always fill in the details later. If I send you a postcard by mail, will you get it? Are you going to move back into the city from your place of work? How is your family? We are all doing well. My greetings to everyone there, and especially to you,

Gazsi

Monday, October 16, 9:00 a.m.[25]
My dear Judit,

It is early morning yet, and I write because I may not be able to write later. Since last Tuesday, we have had air raids every day. Fortunately our district is not bombed every time. When the planes are somewhere else we hear only roaring and rumbling noises from afar and the Saurer cannons shoot only haphazardly. If we hear the shots in the barracks, we rush down into the air-raid shelter. The worst part of all is that after a sleepless night, we have to spend the morning in the shelter. The raids usually last from 10:00 to 2:00. We can sleep from 8:00 to 10:00 and from 3:00 till 5:30. We have to start the next night shift after four-and-a-half hours' sleep.

The whole thing is quite different of course when our area is under attack. The bombs fall as close as 100 metres from us. We are sitting in the *Luftschutzkeller* [air-raid shelter], which, by the way, is a concrete ring covered by two or three feet of earth. I am beside my mother, holding her hand and trying to keep her spirit up. "Look at my face, how quiet it is," I tell her. The noise is thunderous around us. The machines' loud music sounds: zzzzzz.... In the meantime the noise of the guns intermingles: ...boom... ...tatata.... And the most frightening is the whistling of the falling bombs: zhzhzhty...zhzhzhty.... At that time I always warn people around me to open their mouth because the detonation is sometimes so strong that our eardrums almost crack. The ensuing wind sways our coats in the shelter. The people quietly mumble the Shema Yisrael.[26] The shelter rumbles. If an airplane falls down in the neighbourhood it sounds like a siren: oooooopppp.....

And that is just one wave. The sound of the airplanes slowly quiets

---

25 This entry for October 16, as well as the subsequent entry for October 29, were previously translated by Leslie Fazekas, as the originals have since been lost.
26 An important prayer in Judaism; see the glossary.

down. The showering of bombs abates, and the sound of the big guns comes from far away. And then everything gets quiet. But we know that a second and a third wave will follow and the bombs will start coming down again, to this very place. Sure enough, the airplanes start to approach again. We go through this attack with the same trepidation knowing very well that if we survive this one, surely another will come.... If the air raid is over we do not unpack our bags because we expect another air attack in the afternoon. If the afternoon is over, then no more raids will come that day.

At night, we work. (We haven't had any air raids so far at night.) Standing all night is rather exhausting. In the morning we fall into our bed, dead tired, only to wake up two hours later from the noise of the children who rush into the barrack shouting: alarm! alarm! And everything starts all over again. Some people complain about heart trouble already. A day like that wears down the heart of even the bravest of us.

I want to write about another thing. Adjacent to our Lager is the Lager of the political prisoners. Yesterday the weather was good and they went out to their yard and they started to sing. Some of them had such beautiful voices that soon everybody came out of our barrack to see what was happening. We came to the fence that separates the two Lagers and we listened to the song with amazement. Three must have been opera singers, their voices were so beautiful and so articulated. It was a unique experience, making our Sunday evening unforgettable.

My dear Judit,
Sunday, October 29, 4:00 p.m.

I wanted to write in my diary again but — God is my witness — I am so empty that I couldn't produce one normal sentence. So I sat down and I read all the notes I wrote up till now. Some thoughts came to me and so I started to write to me, to you.

First I have to ascertain that even a small stimulus like that can enable me to do some mental work again. It's a long time now since I do not think at all. My only concern is whether the next night will be better or worse than the previous one was. What did the "B" man (the Party's agent) say, or what is the Doctor (our Lager manager) situation.[27] Nothing else. I try sometimes to remember some pre-matriculation materials because I give a lecture to Pista Kovács about Hungarian literature.

I just remember, I don't think. The constant nerve-racking night-work turns me into an animal. And it is okay — otherwise I would be as I was at the beginning of our captivity. I would lament and complain all the time and it would impair and crush me. This way, I hope that I will be able to regenerate.

At the beginning of September I wrote that if I wanted to go to meet you I wouldn't be able to because I was sick. The time is here again, and we will not meet on November 1. Who knows — the place where we are supposed to meet may not exist anymore. Last time, I imagined the street in foggy November. However, I didn't think of the probability that the street doesn't exist anymore. It doesn't matter though anyway, since we established the contact here in Vienna. I wish and I hope that we will meet again, I don't care when. One year has already been wasted.[28]

---

27 The "Party's agent" refers to representatives of the Nazi Party assigned to supervise production in the factory. The doctor refers to the fifty-nine-year-old physician Dr. Sándor Halász, a former public health officer in Szolnok, who was appointed the Jewish commander of the camp.

28 The next part of the diary was lost as well. Leslie's story continues with the letters that follow.

28.11.1944
Dear Judit,

My father tells me that perhaps you will be taken away soon, so this could well be the last opportunity (perhaps the first one?) for me to write to you. Therefore, I'll try and fill you in on all the details, and I expect you to answer in even greater detail, if you can! So far the only note I have received from you is the one you left with Waltner at the hospital. I don't know if there have been other letters from you? Starting in medias res, skipping everything else so I don't forget, with your deportation possibly impending it is vital that I remind you of the arrangement between us: As our agreed-upon dates in September and November have passed, and perhaps so will the one in January, the next ones coming up will be March 1, May 1, July 1 ... etc. If and when it is possible, we will write to the following address in Hungary: Poste Restante F.L. or F.J.,[29] Post Office No. 1, Debrecen. This is also the address where we will meet if we can. Until Tuesday I was hopeful this could happen here in Vienna, but now there is little hope. If there is a way, let me know the name of the new town [you are in] by postcard. They are also going to relocate us, or rather the factory. I believe we are going be retained as workers for the factory in any case, but the word is that we will be moved to a different Lager.

These most important things out of the way, let me say a few words about myself. If you have received some of my letters, I may be repeating myself here and there, but this is not much to worry about. As you know, we work at the Saurer Werke, an automobile factory[30] (located at Wien XI/79 Haidequerstrasse 9 Wohnlager, Lager 4, Baracke 39). We are permanently assigned to the night shift. This is really the only hard

---

29 An abbreviation for Frenkel László and Felberman Judit, following the Hungarian convention of writing family name before first name.

30 See the introduction and Leslie's memoir for more information on Saurer Werke (also spelled as Saurerwerke).

thing about it, I mean only being able to steal a few hours of sleep during the day. (Now it must be around half past three; I only slept from 8:00 till 12:00 in the morning. I will get some more sleep from half past four to six.) Especially when the air-raid sirens come on. When that happens, being roused from your deepest sleep, grabbing your pack, and rushing to the icy bunker shelter are not among the most pleasant things to do. The night shift is from half past seven in the evening to half past six in the morning. My job is to take a cylinder wall of approx. 5 cm radius, 12 cm tall and 1 cm thick, screw it into the machine, and lower the cutter on it that mills it down to the desired dimension in about two to two and a half minutes. I remove the finished piece and insert the next one. I do 120 to 140 of these each night. While the cutter is running I am sitting or standing by the machine. Mostly standing, because I don't feel tired after lying about all day. So this is my job and no more. An eight-year-old would be strong enough to do it.

As I have a lot of time on my hands, I busy myself by collecting the remains of my learning in my mind, which I then commit to paper upon returning to the barrack. Which reminds me, I suspect that I left my biology notes with you. If you still have them, please make sure to send them to me somehow. This would be almost a matter of life or death to me, since I don't have any of my notebooks here, and this one contains all my studies in biology. I am desperate to refresh what I know of at least in this one discipline. But do not send it unless you are absolutely certain that I will get it. You might want to give it or have it given to an attendant named József Auspitz who was transferred there from our barrack. He will find a way to have it delivered to my hand. Don't you forget it! You might as well send a few more pictures, as I only have a couple of them left.

But to return to the factory: It is nice and warm inside all night, so everything would be quite all right, except that the work is boring and demoralizing, even if I manage to occupy myself with my thoughts. Of course, I do talk with those working at the next machine, and I even admit to singing to myself toward the morning, so I often get a hoarse throat by the time I get off. This is my night then, the longer and more taxing part of my day. I only need to add that I have gotten so used to it that I never feel sleepy anymore. Staying up all night was only difficult at first. Not that I don't envy those who sleep soundly while I work. And, after all, staying up at night is hard on your body. It's a good thing that both Gyuri [Leslie's brother] and I are young and able to take it.

Father is by an automatic machine, which means that he has even less to do than I have. Every half an hour he has to measure a finished billet to make sure it is to specification. If it is not, he alerts the technician. Apart from this he has nothing to do. He sits there by the machine, chatting with the others or, God forbid, snatching a few minutes of sleep.

To change the subject to our barrack, there are 114 of us put up here. Only 49 of this number are actually assigned to a job, because women over 45 are not allowed to work and, naturally, women account for the majority. Mom is not working, either. Our barrack is rather agreeable as far as amenities go. Heating is on day and night, and we have plenty of coal. There is a separate bathroom where we can take a bath twice a week. We have a laundry room, a washroom and, to complete the list, even a water closet. We sleep on pallets in plank beds. All in all, our accommodation is cozy and comfortable. It was especially so for us until October while we had a separate room all to ourselves owing to Father's position as Jewish police (Jupo) for the barrack.[31] With the roommates we were less lucky. First of all, none of my friends are around. Second, there is not a single intellect worthy of mention in the barrack with whom I could exchange but a few words about things of science. I do have two friends, both married women. (Don't you get the wrong idea, though!) It is with them, and in truth with them only, that I can talk

---

31 About the controversial role of Jewish police (*Judenpolizei*), see the introduction. There were no such allegations against Andor Frenkel, László's father, or the other four "Jupos" in this camp.

about more serious matters. You don't know them (they are Mrs. Huber and Mrs. Leipnik, who is not from Debrecen) but I will say that they already know you. Both are intelligent women around 30, so we have about ten years between us. Some people among us you might know are Klári Kovács with her family, and Vera Pollák. The rest I have never met before. Not that I know them well now. I prefer to be by myself, reading German, studying mathematics, or writing, whenever I have the time. The others — and that means the girls, as there are only two or three boys in our barrack — are all younger and, unter uns gesagt [between you and me], *rather obtuse. So when the girls gather for a chat, it's mostly about the technicians, and I could not care less about the subject. There are some 10 to 15 girls. Which reminds me, this last Sunday we consulted a Ouija board* [for a séance] *and it told us that the war would be over in two months and then I will meet you again. (I wish I could see it happen now!)*

I needn't tell you that arguments and rows are the order of the day, or that I have never had a falling out with any of them. They can stand on their heads, for all I care. My byword is "splendid isolation," as they say in England. The food is already good. The ration is half a kilo of bread and black coffee in the morning. Three times a week for lunch we get some meat, with jam, margarine, cheese, eggs or a kind of curd cheese substitute alternating weekly. We haven't seen butter at all, but all the more potatoes — almost daily. So dining, so to speak, is out of the question, but the food is satisfactory, if not up to the standards of the meals we have at home (although we cook our own peas, goulash, etc. here whenever we can). For a month and half it was very bad, though.

It is now time to finish this letter, due to shortage of time and paper. By way of an ending, let me just say we have nothing to complain about. Back home our circumstances could be much worse now. We share in the fate of many, many millions. But if next year you and I can be students again, nothing will be amiss. We will be saying what the protagonist in Derű at the Kamara said: We shall draw a veil over the past and move on, as if nothing had happened.[32] *The war, like everything else under the sun, is bound to end someday, and I shall see you then. So far I have been lucky, and I hope it will hold out. And your luck is mine, too. Time goes by fast. After all, the 22 weeks since I last saw you flew by in a second, and if fate sentences us to twice as long (certainly not more), then that won't seem much longer. But what's the point of consoling you? From hearsay I know you look well, as does your mother, and both of you stand up to your destiny. Keep it up! You can rest assured about me. Greetings to you until our reunion, and good health to the relatives. Write to me while still in Vienna, via the hospital (by agency of Forgács or Auspitz), and send a card from the new town to my address. Many greetings again, and don't forget: Fortuna!*

   Laci

30.11.1944
Dear Gazsi,

Apart from the letter you sent with your father, I got your card of October 14, which I answered instantly. I have written to you several times before, but apparently these letters were never delivered to you, obviously because of the inaccuracy of the address as I wrote it down. It would be important for you to tell me the address of the factory before we leave here. We have enough work left to keep us here for about two more weeks. I wouldn't mind it if we wrapped it up, because it's rather hard work, even without the extreme cold weather we are having here. We walk several kilometres to the work site and back each day. For now our job consists of pulling up sugar beets. How this goes is something I hope to be able to tell you in person soon. I could try writing about it

---

32 This is probably a reference to the chamber theatre play *Derű* (*Joy*), written by playwright and dramaturge Ferenc Szécsi in the 1900s.

but the process is too complicated, and you wouldn't be able to visualize it.[33] *The fact of the matter is that we are completely exhausted by the time we get back each night. Pulling potatoes was not much better. Just imagine scuttling about on all fours from morning till night, without a break. But threshing and sheaving wheat was hell in comparison, let me say no more about it. In Vienna I had reported for farm work, thinking eggs, butter and milk, but these daydreams never really came true.*

And now a few words about our so-called "residence," more fittingly termed a stable. There are cracks as wide as my fist in the roof and the walls. They gave us a tiny stove but we had to go door to door in Aspern begging for pipes. Then our dear good landlord announced he was unable to give us any coal as he had very little left himself. All of us had cobbled together makeshift beds for us, only to receive a shipment of bunks today. Lighting is scant as we are allotted only one litre of kerosene a month. This fairy palace provides accommodation for the 45 of us, 35 of whom are assigned to work. This includes my mother and even my grandmother, who has to go out there with the rest, the poor soul, and she is having a hard time of it.

Sharing the place with us are the Róth family, Béla Lusztbaum and his wife, Géza Gáspár and family, Márta Leveles and her family, my uncle Jancsi Liebermann with his folks, and the Heuer family. There are no youngsters apart from my nephew, [John] Róth, and Imre. The only girls are Márta Leveles and Zsuzsi and Éva Róth.

The food is good. We get 400 g [grams] of bread, meat twice a week,

---

33 For another fellow prisoner from Debrecen, Agnes Kaposi, who was twelve in 1944, "harvesting sugar beet was the worst job of all," due to the extreme work conditions. The root "weighing two pounds or more, with huge bushy leaves" was "cemented into the ground by the clay and the frost." Many forced labourers acquired frostbite, with long-lasting consequences. "Your hands are throbbing with pain, your face is covered with mud, but at least the sleet washes away your tears." Agnes Kaposi, *Yellow Star, Red Star* (Manchester: I2i Publishing, 2019), 134–136.

boiled or baked noodles, coffee in the morning, and cheese and jam on Sundays. Like others, we get no butter, only margarine. They gave us our food stamps and we cook meals here at home.

I must stop writing now even though I have some paper and twice as much more to say, because they are sending me from one place to the next (I am a night guard). Some want to wash, others are bothered by the bright light. So what am I to do? I send my best regards to your mother and father, Gyuri and the acquaintances. And special greetings to you until we meet again in a while,

Judith

I do not have your notebook. I haven't forgotten the dates. If you need anything, write to me and I will try to have it sent to you.

[...] This news is catastrophic for us, shattering all my hopes of possibly meeting you here in Vienna.[34] Of course, in my letter I reconfirmed the dates for our rendezvous in Debrecen on January 1, March 1, etcetera... For whatever it is worth, it provides us with a fixed point of reference, and a faint ray of hope that we may see each other again if we survive this conflagration. We cannot fathom how much energy, resourcefulness and sheer effort we have expended to perhaps carry on with the lives we began to build in such serenity and happiness together, and which is now utterly shattered by the fist of war. Yet all it takes is a single bomb, dumb and random, to defeat all hope. But it would be a beautiful thing to meet again — a triumph of endurance, faith and love.

---

34 The diary continues with this partially recovered entry, which Leslie thinks was written on or around December 3. The news Leslie is referring to is likely from Judit's previous letter, dated November 30, 1944, in which she let him know they were to leave the camp in Aspern.

Monday, December 4 at 8:00 a.m.

My dear Judit,

I am now back to the letter I started yesterday, because they told us a show will be held at our barrack and, as you know, I am billed with my series of lectures entitled "Man and His World." The first one went so well that it will continue every Sunday. At least everyone stopped bickering for two hours. I finished at 9:00, so I had no time to resume writing. Let me then pick up where I left off. For 8 or 10 days we had another spell of respite from the air raids, but now they are at it again. Simmering [District XI of Vienna] was among the districts bombed yesterday and the day before. We must have faith that we'll get through it; there is nothing else to ease our lot.

At the factory it's business as usual, no news to report. I have become proficient at the work I do, having learned how to grind my own cutting tool and make the necessary adjustments on my machine. The *Einsteller* [foreman] has stopped checking on me all night. We leave each other alone, and this makes for a better, more relaxing night shift for both of us. I spend the time thinking to myself or talking to others. I have developed the habit of writing down a few words about the hallowed day we parted ways, and perhaps the one we will meet again.

We are into the sixth month [of separation]. Time has flown, and there is no use in lamenting it. The pain will be washed away by time, this great healer that cures all, and we can find comfort in the absolute certainty that it cannot last as long as we have been here already. And we haven't died from it. So it would be all right, except for those bombs! We have plenty of food. For instance, I have five and a half kilos of bread stashed away in my cloth bag as we speak, saved for harder times from days when I did not need more. It must be around 11 o'clock now. I am lying in bed. The boys have stopped by for a chat. At least I did not think of eating while we talked.

[handwritten on back]
Judith Felbermann
c/o Hans Oberleuthner
Landwirt
Wien XXII.148
Ehrensteing 9

11.12.1944
Dear Judith,

My father is going to the hospital again tomorrow, so I am writing again. Let me begin with what matters most, as usual. I understand from your letter to Father that you have written several postcards to me, but I never received any. In our Lager nobody gets postcards, they always get lost somehow. So when you let me know your new address, please don't just send a card to me (though let's try anyway) but also write to the name of József Auspitz at the hospital. (You must know the hospital's address.) There is always someone going there from our Lager to bring your letter to me. Do everything you can to remain in Vienna. Of course, I am aware that our fate does not depend on us in the least bit hereabouts, but man probiert, as the French say [sic, German, one tries]. What matters is that I get hold of your address one way or an-other. Then I will find a way to let you know if my own address happens to change.

Since I explained the basic details of our life here in my previous letters — as you did in yours — this one consists of mere chit-chat. You already know how good we have it here, and I also know about your life up to this point. One thing I can say for sure is that we were luckier than you in where we ended up. Our living quarters are better by far than yours. Here we live in a warm, heated barrack in orderly conditions, and even if the food is inferior, it tastes better than the most delicious noodles if you eat it when you are frozen to the bone and ex-hausted from all that hard work. If only I didn't have to be surrounded by such low people. I hardly speak to anyone around me throughout the day. At first, it was very difficult to get used to being grounded like this. During the first 3 or 4 days I just slept all the time when I was not working, amid all these strangers, some of whom I thought had a chance to become precious company for me in our bleak captivity. I was harshly disillusioned fast. Suffice it to say, my little brother boasts the highest education in our barrack.

For the first 8 days we did not go to the factory, and I spent my time lying about in the front yard or in the room, thinking of you all and our friends, wondering where you were. I thought no place on earth could be worse than this narrowly fenced barrack. I was blaming myself for not having been able to wait for you. If we had managed to stick together, perhaps it would have been easier.

Apart from solitude, my mood was aggravated by the poor food. There were days when I was unable to eat my lunch or dinner. We were kept going only by the scant leftovers we had managed to salvage from home. I wrote bitter letters to my far-away aunt in Constantinople, Turkey, which at least made time pass more quickly, and I could get things off my chest.[35] As long as I was busy putting my bitter, whirling thoughts into smooth, clear sentences, I didn't consider my situation that unpleasant. I was distressed even by the thought of having to stay here for a month, because at the time I didn't think it would be more than that. The first days passed as if on leaden feet. The hardest thing to get used to was the captivity. The brickyard had been a breeze in comparison. July 10, the first day we went to the factory, brought a little welcome change. I was curious about the machines and had the opportunity to talk with strangers, people from Italy, France, Greece, Poland, Russia [the Soviet Union] *and Germany, about the customs and national characteristics in their respective countries. And I slept during the day whenever I could. Sleeping put me back at home, among dear friends and relatives. They had never been as nice as now, like good health for a sick man.*

---

35 See the footnote to the diary entry of August 10.

Then time passed, gradually. At first I counted the days, later the weeks. The days passed in a flash as time went by. Faster than the nights, which seemed never-ending at first. Fortunately, the supervisors at the factory would condone people snatching a few minutes of sleep here and there. Sometimes I would sleep 3 or 4 hours all together. This was the sleeping time I could count on. But the nights were studded with latent sleep as well — asleep while sitting down, working, even while talking to others. I would work away with my eyes wide open, dreaming long dreams. This was my routine for many many weeks, until my body got used to staying up all night. I never got much sleep if any during the day. In the morning we usually had air raids, and in the afternoon, you could not sleep for the heat and the flies. I was longing for cool weather to set in. Summer turning into autumn finally granted that prayer. The nuisance of minutes was compensated for by the quick passage of time. The minutes were long because they were uniform, unable to soar on fascinating events. But the weeks went by fast precisely because of the uneventful days that failed to leave a mark. Two or three weeks here amounted to spending a single day or even a single hour at home. On Sundays I would think back on the past week and find nothing except the vague memory of sleeping through the night in bed. Is this what they call a long week?

What else can I write? Habit has made life easier eventually. We have gotten used to the food, even to captivity and constant work. Over time, though, the food improved by a great deal. Our daily ration of bread has been raised from 330 to 450 grams. I also got used to not speaking to people, learning to turn to study whenever I feel bored. I now have a German dictionary and write to my auntie less frequently (although I wish you and I could read that correspondence one day). Drowsiness at night is a thing of the past. I feel as refreshed at night as I used to be in the morning. It's just the air raids, which have become more severe. I don't know if I have told you, but our Lager has been hit by 6 bombs, one of them just 40 metres away from our barrack behind which there is a shelter for 110 people. But you can gradually get used to all of this, believe it or not. And we are slowly getting used to the

*idea of death, so it will not come unexpected. But I am being facetious
here. I very much want to live, and not merely stay alive. If we are to
suffer so much, enduring an unimaginably harsh fate (not to mention
the "insolence of office"[36]), it is only because we know deep down that
what comes after is a happier life. Hamlet's dagger must be kept from
our hearts not just by the fear of the dream that awaits us on the other
side but also because of what life has to offer on this side. From these
allusions to Hamlet I should now switch to the faint ray of hope in
The Tragedy of Man that is nevertheless more than powerful enough
to prevent the extinction of all humanity as we know it, with all those
lives that are hardly less miserable than our own.[37] (This was a rather
convoluted formulation of the kind I have not written for a long while;
lucky me that I didn't get entangled in it myself.)*

*To make a long story short, we are living in times when the deepest
despair can be followed by long-awaited liberation any minute. This is
not the optimism of a man fallen on hard times but a fact borne out by
experience. We are clearly in profound trouble for the moment, even
God Almighty could not deny it. My old diaries — if I had them around
— contain frequent mentions of my wish for a youth full of struggle as
a precondition for a rich, beautiful adulthood. This wish of mine seems
to have been granted by destiny, except that the real struggle will come
after the war; I feel it in my bones. Perhaps all this was both necessary
and inevitable to guarantee that I did not have too cushy a life in my
younger years. One thing is certain: We will not pick up, and will not
want to pick up, where we left off 7 months ago. Our subsequent lives,
no matter how hard, will be richer in experience, battles, victories and
disillusionment. This is just to say that our troubles may loom large
at the moment, but the future is enticing — much more enticing than
we can imagine here and now. I have been prattling on too much, but*

---

36 A quote from Shakespeare's *Hamlet* (Act III, Scene I).
37 A reference to the last scene in Imre Madách's nineteenth-century play *The Tragedy of Man*, a classic read in Hungary.

babbling had reason to it, one of historical chronology, or at least so I tried. I have written the least about our present life, only because I have not much else to say about it. The days go by fast, and with every passing one of them, we have one less to go. Yet the end seems so far away!

We have just been told there is a Luftgefahr [imminent air raid]. *So far, we have made it to the end of this day. Let's wait and see what tomorrow brings. I must take a break from writing now. There is some room left on the page so I may continue later. — Now I am back to it after lunch, still chewing on my slice of bread with jam. There was a big air raid over Vienna, but luckily quite some distance from us. The only thing of interest was a paratrooper who landed not far from us. Then we had lunch. It is now past three o'clock, and we have to get up at half past five for dinner, so I am going to bed. I pray to God that this is not my last letter to you.... In any case, write to this address and also address it to Auspitz, but be careful! By the way, thank you for that package. We were just as upset as you were when we found out it had gotten lost on the way under such mysterious circumstances. But it is not an irreplaceable loss. Many greetings until we write to and see each other again,*
Laci

Sunday, December 17
My dear Judit,

I normally study on Sundays and write on Mondays, but given that I skipped last week, I decided to make up for it today. The other day I was talking to Klári at the factory, and she asked me if I was still in love with Judit. She knows how I feel about her, and obviously expected me to answer yes. Yet, I told her that I'd been thinking about it lately. This was the most sincere and most rational answer I could give her. The fate we share does not bind us together, and the memories we shared are all becoming blurred. The picture I have of you is no longer as sharp as it was before, and that small, bespectacled face, too, must have changed since. It's no use denying that time, the great healer, will wash away all. When we parted ways, I was curious to find out whether an ardent love such as ours was also subject to the adage "loin des yeux, loin du cœur." [Far from the eyes, far from the heart.] Till now I haven't thought this could be the case with us, but if it goes on like this much longer, I am afraid that it could become true. I will never forget her a hundred percent, but one thing is certain: We will have to begin everything from the start. The time we meet again will be like meeting for the first time. It is possible that we will not find each other attractive at all. (But it's all the more likely that yes, I would find you very attractive if you were here with me now!) Our first kiss will be the first kiss, and we will probe into each other's minds as if we have never met before. Seven months can bring profound change, and these particular two months certainly have for us, not only in our circumstances but in our very outlook on life. We have new feelings. We have become new persons all around and will continue to change. But I have no misgivings about it. We will be discovering many unfamiliar traits, finding each other interesting, and it is even possible that after this hiatus our love will soar to hitherto unexplored heights.

As for the rest, I have nothing new to report. I now operate my machine in total independence, grinding the cutting tools myself, and I am on good terms with my *Einsteller*. My nights have become bearable, indeed calm and peaceful, and I have miraculously learned to find the company of Mrs. Huber and Mrs. Leipnik agreeable. They, too, seem to have grown to respect me and like me instead of making me feel merely tolerated. I know this from what Nusi told me the other day. She said she could feel I had been putting more distance between us lately and wanted to know why. She misses the heartfelt and edifying conversations we used to have. I said I liked these exchanges very much myself and would be pleased to resume them. We continue to have a fair number of alerts, but no air raids so far. We will see!

Sunday, December 24 at 15:00 [3:00 p.m.]
My dear Judit,

We have three days off, and I am afraid of boredom, being all by myself. If only you could be around, my dear Judit! But for all I know you may no longer be in Vienna, let alone here with me. The 14 days your uncle said your job will be over in have long passed. Here we stand again, sightless in the dark, two lovers who do nothing but search for each other endlessly, as if spellbound and doomed, like those against whom everything has conspired to prevent them from attaining what they are striving for. You on one shore, I on the other, both in the utter unknown, with a great body of water between us. Whether it is a stream, a river or an ocean we cannot know, but for now it surely seems impossible for us to swim across. Perhaps this large body of water will freeze over later in the winter, and we can walk across without even wetting our feet.

It is now Christmas-time, and we miss the usual vacation sorely. Tuesday night we will have to go and pick up our shift at the factory. We only have two nights to sleep here at home, tonight and tomorrow. Then the endless string of days at the factory will continue.

If I think back on the year we are leaving behind, my Judit, I feel like crying. Last year, our great love was nearing fulfillment. I remember, back in Debrecen, you had this fellow Laci Barna around, but even though you might have had some good times together, your heart wasn't in it. I could hardly wait to make my visit to your place as a house tutor, if only for a brief hour, and I could feel that you too were waiting for the moment when our lips would meet for a first kiss. It hurt my feelings when you had a new dress made for yourself to please Laci. I would go skating often in those days, and I promised to teach you before the end of the year. Hey, we have skidded off that track badly, haven't we, my Judit? I don't want to skate and skid anymore; I would be happy to have a swim together now. And I entertain eager plans for hiking, for striving toward a peak from the deep valleys below. How wonderful that struggle together will be, my Judit, as the two of us forge upwards, fighting against the elements! How many severe blows do we still have to endure before our hard toil and bitter experiences will be compensated by sweet kisses? We will be fighting a slow but tough battle for each other together, shoulder to shoulder. I shall be your encouragement and you my helper. The horrible life we have here will seem light compared to what is in store for us. But the future will be infinitely more joyous, because we will be together and never leave each other again. It will be just the two of us, and together you and I shall be stronger than the entire world.

We have a long, long way to go before this ordeal is over, or so it seems to me today. Fate demands an exorbitant price for happiness. "We pay for everything, for every single moment."[38] Half a year has flown by already. What lies ahead will be long, but it will be easy to draw a veil over the past. We shall pass over it in silence and forget about it all, as the protagonist in *Joiselle* does.[39] What is a year lost compared to a life we will have won? If we get out of here, we shall face a life we have fought for and won, a life with open gates for us to conquer. Hold out, I encourage myself, as I encourage you in the unknown distance, my little heroine, my love. We have paid the price and shall win the prize, which will be happiness together.

Tuesday, December 26 at 10:00 a.m.
My dear Judit,

I am lying in bed, and I am not going to get up unless they sound the air-raid alert. I am writing to tell you about what happened in our barrack yesterday. Here, in the middle of nowhere, we received two

---

38 From a song in the popular Hungarian operetta *Mária főhadnagy (Lieutenant Mary)* by Jenő Huszka (1942).
39 A reference to the play *Joyzelle* written by the Belgian playwright Maurice Maeterlinck (1903).

visitors, Aunt Gizi and her company [her husband]. They came to make us happy, but they only brought sadness to many of us in the barracks. You see, they are allowed to go out to town, get paid 80 marks a month, and were even given an extra 25 marks as a Christmas gift. In short, they enjoy almost total freedom, like the Russians [Soviet POWs] do here. I cannot begin to tell you how much such a degree of freedom would mean to me. I could have visited you any number of times over the past half a year. I would have gladly sacrificed my sleeping time during the day just to see you once in a while. In this way, our love would have been sustained by burning fresh memories rather than by sheer longing. But there is nothing to be done. We are now living here, utterly doomed. We do not yet understand what good will come of it, but it ain't over till it's over, as they say. Then it will be our turn to curse the day we got here. I am not saying another word now, and I won't allow myself to feel depressed by everything I see around me. I only hope we live to see the day when we can reflect back on these times and decide which of us fared better. Here they started heating the water closet. Yesterday I spent some time studying and tutoring others. Today it's writing only for me, although if I have some time left in the morning I may study a little German before I do my toilet [wash up]. The afternoon is strictly reserved for sleeping.

To: László Frenkel
Wien XI/ 79 Haidequerstrasse Österr. Saurer Werke
Wohnlager Lager 4 Baracke 39
From: Judith Felbermann Wien XXI. Floridsdorf
Kuenburggasse 1. Schule, Floor I/5

30.12.1944

Dear Gazsi,

My uncle Jancsi is going to the hospital this week and I will be sending a letter with him. I am afraid this will be the last time, as he is not required to make any more visits. In any case, I will write you postcards, both in your name and via József Auspitz, and I expect you to reply right away, to my new address. Try making an appointment with the dentist's office here. You may have a bad tooth somewhere, and if you don't — well, just say that you think you do. I am quite sure you will manage.

And now onto something about our move to the new place. At noon on Thursday, when we got back from work, we were told to pack as we were leaving at one o'clock [to Floridsdorf]. I had a very bad feeling about it when I found out. I don't know if you have heard, but this particular district in Vienna is subject to constant air raids, almost daily. Jews in that district have been sent from one Lager to the next three or four times. So we were about to be relocated to the worst possible place, and at a time when our life here has just begun to get better — with no work,[40] improved food, well-heated rooms, and in peace. The Slovakian girls had been taken somewhere else, and we moved into their three-room apartment, all 21 of us. The others stayed in the barrack. Unfortunately, this royal tenure turned out to be short-lived.

So we packed, loaded our baggage on the carts that had come in, and set out on the road again, like so many times before, to an unknown place where strangers awaited us, toward new dangers. Luckily it wasn't too cold. If it had been, we would have frozen to death during

---

40 There was no work because the agricultural labour was seasonal, and thus practically over by this time.

the two-hour journey. When we arrived at our destination, we were greeted by ruins everywhere. There is practically not a single undamaged building here. Even the school, where we were put up in a chilly room, has half of it missing. For the time being they gave us no beds to sleep in. The place was a huge mess, loud with tumult and bickering. It was snowing in large flakes outside. All I wanted was to go for an aimless walk, as was my wont to do back home.

I had learned to take freedom too much for granted in Aspern. Here, however, all the gates are locked. I just walked up and down the corridors, in and out of one room to the next. I was yearning to get out of here, to escape to a better place, but could do nothing about it, and the sense of helplessness was exasperating. I felt completely alone among 500 people. In my sorrow I went to bed in my day clothes and wept endlessly. I miss Aspern, even though I had suffered and worked hard over there. I miss all the people I grew accustomed to there, and I miss the fields, the streets, the houses and the barns. I miss everything and everyone I had to leave behind. Eventually, I cried myself to sleep. I had to spend the whole next day making rounds to visit people because our room remained freezing cold despite the heating.

The food is bad and the portions meagre. Not once since we came here have I been able to eat what they gave us. Fortunately, we had brought along some potatoes, carrots and onions from the village. I have no idea what we are going to do when all of it is gone. We have not been going out to work all day. Instead we take turns, for hours at a time, clearing the rubble across from the school. This job would be child's play compared to pulling sugar beet, were it not for the bitter cold.[41] *I am sure we will handle this part of it. What I am a little scared*

---

41 Clearing rubble could also involve hard work and serious danger because of collapsing ruins and unexploded bombs, as well as the dreadful task of carrying dead bodies.

*of are the air raids, although nothing of the kind has happened since we
moved here. But one day this whole circus will come to an end, and we
shall meet again. I am longing to see you. I hope it will happen before
the year is out. We suffered so badly, went through so much trouble this
past year, that I must feel the next one can only bring us beauty and joy.
Do everything you can to come and see us…*

*Till then, wishing you and the family a Happy New Year,
Judith*

Sunday, December 31 at 8:30 a.m.
My dear Judit,

If my keeping a diary has been reduced to writing on special days
only (and each Sunday is special, in that it was on this day of the
week that we last saw each other), today I shouldn't be doing anything other than writing and writing and writing. And this day is at
once another important anniversary: It was precisely one year ago,
on December 31, 1943, that our paths first crossed. So it has been one
year that we have been joined together, even if we are apart for now.
Ultimately it would not matter if that preordained first encounter had
happened a day sooner or later. As it happens, we have just closed the
chapter on one year — mine so productive and successful in terms
of all the new knowledge I absorbed. Now we embark on our second
year, amid profoundly changed circumstances.

It must have been around this time of the day that the doorbell of
the apartment at Vörösmarty [street] 14 rang. It was Judit showing up
for our date; we had agreed to go out to the woods to take some pictures. She had an exercise class at 11:00 and I wanted to do my skating
later in the morning, so I picked up my skates and camera, and we
took the streetcar to the woods [the Nagyerdő, Great Forest Park].
We got off at the Vigadó and started roaming around. We walked to

the small hill by the pond, where I took pictures on the footbridge and of the two of us sitting on a bench with our arms around each other. It was past 10:30 when we decided we couldn't put off leaving a minute longer. You said you were very cold. I wasn't, so I unbuttoned my overcoat and told you to huddle up to me. We held each other tight there among the freezing woods. Our lips were close, and we kissed. I felt a dizziness come over me. Then a policeman strolled by, and we fluttered apart. You caught your streetcar at the university, I jumped on the streetcar step after you, and we quickly agreed to go see a movie together in a few days, when Laci Barna would finally leave for home. The streetcar lunged forward, and I stayed on that step for a while (I had a monthly pass in any case), holding on with one hand and my briefcase in the other. As I finally jumped off around the bend, I slipped and fell down. It was a nasty big fall that left scabs on my knees for a month. I cursed the day you were born as I scrambled to my feet! To think what you got me into! Then I did go to the skating rink but couldn't get you out of my mind. I was musing over that kiss, the very first kiss of my life, which would engender a string of hundreds and hundreds of more kisses to come. I had never kissed before because I knew, and kept telling myself, that kissing a woman was a serious choice for me. I would become engaged to the woman I kiss. Therefore, my dear Judit, what we performed that day was nothing less than an act of engagement. That is why I remember that day as faithfully as I do.

I returned home around 2 o'clock. I grabbed a quick lunch then went to see Peti [Peter Kálmánczi]. (Here I should write an aside about Zsuzsi. That one was a peculiar romance in its own right.)[42] We made the irrevocable decision to have a New Year's Eve party. We walked from store to store buying bottles of wine and *pálinka*

---

42 Leslie refers to Peti and Zsuzsi in his memoir on pages 103–104.

[Hungarian fruit spirits] and got tickets to the movie theatre for the night. Then I went home, studied for a while, had my dinner and read up on my chemistry. I did not want to waste a single minute without study. (As it turns out, I have spent thousands of minutes of my life without studying since then…)

The New Year's Eve show was being aired on the radio. Mrs. Schank was staying in. Around 10 o'clock I changed my clothes and went to Peti's place. We drank until 11:00, then it was movie time until 1:00. (At midnight all the lights went out and a man came on stage to wish the audience a happy new year, making all of us laugh out loud.) After 1 o'clock we were rejoined by Jancsi Feldmann, and we partied until the wee hours.

I never saw you a second time that day, as you spent New Year's Eve in Laci's company, but you and I were together in our thoughts the whole time. At least, you were on my mind all night long. So this was the story of that memorable day, the day of our engagement, as we bade farewell to a fine year and stepped into a sad new one.

Interestingly, every New Year's Eve I would ask myself the same question that seemed so obvious to ask: Are we all going to live to see the next year, together in good health and spirits, as in the old year? That night, however, I had no doubt that nothing could come between us, that the road ahead of us would be an easy one. And today? It sends shivers down my spine just to think of the next New Year's Eve and the year that lies ahead. Is it possible it will find me reduced to decaying bones? In the past, I would wish for the next New Year's Eve to find us together as before, a company celebrating in good spirits. Now I wish only that it simply finds us alive, if separated. But what the new year will bring this time I dare not even think about. We have so little agency in controlling our own destiny that it is futile to make advance calculations.

Although the direction our life will take is out of our hands, I am certain that the new year will bring many changes. On New Year's Eve

I have the habit of glancing back at the past year. Such a glance would fill 100 pages this time, and I do not have that much paper to write on. So here is a shorthand version. At the beginning of the year, I whiled away the time mostly with Nebu [reference unknown]. January 3: a day to remember; Judit leaves her mark on every month. February: my last good month, full of fun, the baths and a lot of study. March 19: our German allies march in. April: ecstatic swoon of love with Judit. May 1 to June 2: good times in Haláp, with Peti, Tomi, Horo [Horovitz] and Janka.[43] June 2: the bombing of Debrecen. To June 16: clearing rubble from the ghetto.[44] June 16 to 28: the brickyard. Never been so resourceful before, inspired by Judit. Helping each other a lot. Then the cattle car, an unconscious spell with Judit beside me. July 1: Strasshof, the first air raid, the day we are separated. July 2: the Vienna hub. We are assigned to Saurer's here. I have been working the night shift since July 10. Going hungry much of the time at first, and longing for Judit.

By now we have gotten used to this life; Judit is with me forever. And now here is this New Year's Eve, a holiday I am going to distinguish from other days by simply sleeping through the night. My expected schedule for today: writing in the morning, save for a possible air raid; studying after lunch, then getting dressed and enjoying my free time. If a show on stage is scheduled for the night, we will prepare for that in the afternoon. Finally, the highlight of the day: going to bed to get a good night's sleep. And tomorrow we will step into a new year, perhaps one even more crucial and life-changing than the one behind us. May good Fortune stand by my side!

---

43 Out of this group of young men, only Leslie and "Horo" (Gábor Horovitz) survived the Holocaust. "Janka" refers to Leslie's classmate András Frank (1925–1944). Regarding the fates of Peti and Tomi, see the memoir.

44 The ghetto inmates were taken to clear rubble in the bombed sections of the city, not in the ghetto, which was not bombed.

Sunday, January 14, 1945, at 16:00 [4:00 p.m.]
My dear Judit,

We are well into the new year now as I revisit my diary for the first
time. Not much has happened here in the meantime, but I believe
all the more with you over there. I hear you have been transferred to
Floridsdorf [District x x i of Vienna] but nothing further about the
nature of your work or circumstances. I don't even know your exact
address. In any event, I was elated to learn you stayed in Vienna. I
haven't given up the hope that, God willing, we may meet while both
of us are still in the city. Oh, if only you could come and see me once,
my Judit! People from other Lagers are allowed to go on a leave. Last
Sunday we had 6 visitors from other Lagers, among them a vivacious,
animated girl of 18 by the name of Éva Krausz. (When she was told I
was courting you, she complimented me on my good taste. I was terribly proud!) They came around 10:00 in the morning and left around
3:00. We spent a very nice time with them.

Whenever I find myself in a slightly better frame of mind, when
for a moment I snap out of this seven-month delirium, I am horrified
to think of dying, of being deprived of so many wonderful moments
of life to come, if I were hit by a stray bomb. I may have lived long
enough to experience a great deal, from joy to intense suffering, from
hard-won victories to bitter defeat, perhaps more than many people's
share in a lifetime, but I am still young with a life ahead of me — the
real life, the greatest battle of all. But all of this now seems so vague,
so distant, as never before. I seldom fret about living or dying anymore. Let come what may. Compared to not having been born at all,
my life so far is a pure gain. Dying is just a return to Nirvana. Simple
as that, isn't it? The war has devoured millions of lives, why should
I be the exception? In any case, we haven't had a single air raid this
year. It would not be nice to have to rush to the cellar in this cold. It
would be particularly hard on poor Father, who is seriously ill. He is
suffering all the time, moaning, or rather, wailing in pain, through

the night. If only he could feel better! It is terrible to see him so help-less in his torment, without any medication or diet, as if we were still cavemen! When is this all going to end?

Sunday, January 21 at 21:00 [9:00 p.m.]
My dear Judit,

Many of us might face big changes over the coming days. It is ru-moured that the factory may relieve us of our duties. I would be happy beyond words if this were true, because I've gotten bored of it, with its meals, 11-hour night shifts and everything else. But the *Einstellers* would be reluctant to train new people for the position, so they want us to move with the works. So, I believe we are going to be retained by the factory.

Today Simmering has been hit by a massive air raid, with 3 huge bombs falling very close to us. Another two have not even exploded yet. The whole shelter was shaking. All the while, Mother and Father stayed behind in the barrack because Father had very bad spasms and was unable to come down. Father is terribly sick, and it is even more terrible to think of him being moved to another Lager in this condition.

As for myself, I wouldn't mind working outside if need be. The winter is not very cold, even comfortable if you keep working. The seasons came and went without us noticing here in the factory. Of course we knew when it was summer, autumn or winter outside, but the distinctions became blurred. Back at home, life in the winter was entirely, radically different from life in the summer. The winter was marked by studies, well-heated rooms, cozy nooks, and the laughter of cheerful company by the fireside. In the summer, we would go to the baths or for long hikes outdoors, just enjoying our vacation. Here it's just the factory and nothing else, be it summer or winter. Sleeping during the day regardless of the season. Well, perhaps the summer was worse for the stinging flies. Other than that, everything is always the same here. Living like this, even for a minute, is not sustainable. It's all sleep or work. 11 hours of work (13 with getting ready and travel) plus 2 hours for lunch and dinner. That makes 15 hours, and then you need 9 hours to sleep.

Many of us do not even have the time to talk to others. If we worked during the day, at least we would have our evenings to ourselves. It goes without saying that no newspapers are allowed here. If we get too bored at work, we have a little fun by pulling a joke on one or two unlucky fellows, just to have our whole group laugh at him. Once we told Mrs. Fellner and Mrs. Silberstein that a certain number of us could be transferred on the request of a dairy farm. All we had to do was sign up for the new job with the *Meister*. The two good ladies quickly started scheming against the others to get ahead, and eventually managed to "sign up" with the *Meister*. Of course, the *Einstellers* and the *Meister* had all been in on our secret little game.

The first half of winter is now gone. We have another week to go until it's February, then spring will be around the corner, and by summer the war may be over. What is a year in the times we live in, when even a human life is not too much to sacrifice? Except for those who yield it.

Tuesday, January 23 at 18:00 [6:00 p.m.]
My dear Judit,

The reason I am writing on this unusual day of the week is that I received a letter from you in the afternoon [Judit's letter dated December 30, 1944], and I want to record my impressions while they are still fresh. Finally, Father was admitted to the hospital for tests and possibly in-patient care. Those who went in with him and came back brought your letter to me. I find it wonderful and very sad at the same time. I admit that I positively liked it. I thought there was not a single unnecessary sentence in it. You are telling me of having lived in relative freedom (under the circumstances, that is), 21 of you in a well-heated three-room apartment and with decent food, so overall you had a good life in Aspern. Now that you have been transferred, it is hard to get used to the strangers around you and the new circumstances, and you are struggling to overcome the initial difficulties. I know how you feel. When we first came here, I felt so forlorn and bereft in this barrack for 120 that often I just wanted to cry. The only consolation and the only poison I had consisted of my memories. And the most wonderful, most intensely burning memories of all were of the two of us who share them. I was still so ardently in love with you that I almost died of it. I have been hardened and gotten used to this life since then — to the solitude, the silence, the abandonment. Even my memories have stopped harassing me.

The machine I operate at the factory has taught me many things: how to bear it all and wait one's time without stirring, how to shake off the slings of fate,[45] everything that hurts. What we have turned into during the past seven months is not animals but machines, numb organisms. It is hard at first, isn't it, my Judit? Man can be transformed into anything, as easily to an animal as to a mechanism, but this metamorphosis is difficult and takes some time. Eventually, you will become jaded, too. As the initial physical discomforts slowly recede and you manage to get a bed and a warmer place to sleep, your feelings, drives and desires will become less intense. Slowly, step by step — but before long, as we measure time here — you will become like me, like the rubble you clear. And I do want you to be like me in this one thing: No matter how desensitized I am now, I have never forgotten nor could ever forget you. My love for you is just as persevering, perhaps a lot more persevering, if less ardent and painful, than when our tribulations began.

----

45 Although not a verbatim quote, this is most likely an allusion to the well-known soliloquy that starts with the phrase "To be, or not to be," from Act III, Scene I of William Shakespeare's *Hamlet*. The exact line is, "The slings and arrows of outrageous fortune."

Sunday, January 28 at 17:00 [5:00 p.m.]
My dear Judit,

I have just finished writing a letter to you. A few more words for now, then I am going to read some German. Tomorrow I will be studying mathematics. All week we have been wondering if we will move along with the factory. Now it seems we will be going [to work] underground, transported by motor vehicles back and forth. These night shifts are getting to me. I get these strong heart palpitations during the day, so it would be nice to switch to a daytime job. Even if it is hard work, I wouldn't mind. Those exempt from work so far have recently been listed, so they might have to go to work from now on. If they do, it will be better than the night shift at the factory, though.

28.01.1945
My dear Judit,

On Tuesday this week I received your letter dated the 30th last month. Father is now sick, something with his stomach. He is hospitalized for an examination and perhaps treatment. He was the one who sent the letter home; maybe now we can communicate more easily through him. If someone from your Lager visits the hospital, make sure they find Father. Address your letter to Auspitz, as I won't get it delivered to my name. I have no access to your Lager because we have our dentistry on the Malzgasse, not far from Mariahilferstrasse, in the Lager of [illegible word].[46] *But I am surprised why you never visited us from Aspern if you were so free there. We received many visitors from other camps. Alas, we cannot do this as we have been kept behind locked gates for two months. But what I really want to do now is reply to your letter, which affected me most profoundly.*

---

46 Leslie refers to the hospital of the Viennese Jewish community at Malzgasse 16, District II of Vienna.

Your letter was full of sadness, resignation. Very plaintive. But I must say it was also beautiful. It is for a reason that they say, and it is an established fact, that grief, the hurt of the body and — with or without it — the hurt of the soul, produces works of far greater classical purity than happiness ever can. In your letter I felt there was not a single superfluous word or sentence. It is an elegy crystallized in torment, ending with a flicker of hope. It made me reflect on my own situation as I read it — the state I was in two months ago, and the questions I asked myself. Back then, I was still living under the spell of wonderful memories from Debrecen and Haláp, and when the small garden gate closed behind me that had so safely kept me from the world outside, what people call life, I felt terribly abandoned among complete strangers. Hungry and filled with painful, burning memories of people who have ended up so far away from me. I felt I could not endure this for long. You can never deny yourself, never give up your dreams. Your ambition, your desire to act will constantly drive you toward the new, the mysterious, the unknown. Under the circumstances, I felt like a dead man. Dead, but with senses intact. Months passed, at first slowly, then faster. Step by step, what we had thought intolerable became routine. The scraps of food, the confinement, the solitude. I grew more and more desensitized. I had a good mentor to rely on: my machinery. A silent machine incapable of feeling or motion, who only needs to be fed to go about its duty. Without sense or desire, it lives on in a serene world of its own, unperturbed by good or bad. And I was a good student this time, as I usually am. Gradually, the two machines fused in me: The one that had remained in the factory for good became one with the other who would go to see it and sit by its side from evening till dawn. Now that my own days and nights are calmer, I no longer brew any plans for the future and I quit thinking, shutting off everything that hurts or causes discomfort. Since then, I have been living happily. You are still at the beginning. Aspern was not good schooling.[47] *The new place seems better. You will just need time to get used to it. Way to start, as they say. But, eventually, beds will be put in, the room will be warmer, the food more edible. The sooty ruins, the rearing firewalls will suck you in, as did the endless meadows, the drafty barns and all those little rattling machines. And the newcomers, who seem such strangers at first, mere indifferent objects moving about, will infiltrate your life, becoming part of your daily routine and often leaving pleasant memories behind. But my words of consolation may come late, as you probably found your own consolation as soon as you put the first difficulties behind you. If you haven't, it will come. I just wanted to tell you that nothing is as intolerable as it may seem at first.*

Another thing I can tell you is that there is one district that was bombed even harder than Floridsdorf: Simmering.[48] *Suffice it to say that our Lager has been hit by 11 bombs. Only one or two out of ten buildings escaped being damaged. The roof of our barrack has been shattered twice but so far, we have not been hurt in any way. Good luck seems to be standing by me for now, or so I would like to hope. We must be preserved, we must survive this cataclysm. I feel and know this necessity, and I am confident that we will make it. When it will all end nobody knows, but each passing day brings us closer to reunion, to returning home, to a new life. We got here last July. If everything goes well, we may be home by July this year. What are we going to go through till then? Well, we will tell each other while sitting in a peaceful room, and the more horrible our stories, the happier we shall be for having been rescued from such perils.*

---

[47] Leslie clarified what he meant by this: that Aspern did not teach Judit to tolerate the inevitable suffering.

[48] Actually, as industrial districts, both Simmering and Floridsdorf were heavily bombed.

I don't have much else to report. A while ago they were supposed to take us away from here, as the factory was hit by a bomb, but our division was relocated to an underground facility quite far from here. I believe that's where we are going to commute every night for work. The Lager itself will stay. Of course, nothing is certain here. Otherwise I am well, I am in good health, have even put on some weight, and have been in better spirits lately. I will send a postcard to your address and will be awaiting yours sent via the hospital. And do visit me if you still can.

Wishing you good luck until we meet again soon,

Laci

Kisses and greetings to relatives and [partially illegible due to torn page].

Monday, February 5 at 21:00 [9:00 p.m.]
My dear Judit,

It's awful that I hardly slept at all this past week. If you were told you can get by with so little rest you wouldn't believe it. Let me take tally: Monday afternoon 3 to 6, Tuesday 8 to 14 (the longest), Wednesday 8 to 12, Thursday 8 to 11, Friday 17 to 18, Saturday 8 to 11, Sunday 6 to 10. That's 24 hours in seven days, an average of three and a half hours per day. If I lived like this back at home, I would have lost 5 kilos in just two days. Here, I simply felt tired, but today even that sense of exhaustion is gone. Tonight we will be back at it again. The reason I slept so little, if at all, is that Friday morning we were moved to barrack 44 by the highway. Here we are put up in separate rooms in groups of eight, which is better. The only hitch is that I share a room with my aunt and her children, who happen to be naughty as hell.

February 12 at 9:00 a.m.

My dear Judit,

Not for a moment have I doubted your love and fidelity, just as my own feelings have never been in doubt for a minute. When one day I wrote that, after seven months of separation, it must be natural for me not to feel so much in love with you anymore, this came from an intellectual experience rather than one of actual emotion. In reality, I loved you just as much as before, and my self-doubt was nothing if not the evidence of this love. Your visit yesterday demonstrated it eloquently. I am grateful to you for it, because it startled me out of my lethargy and sense of being death-bound following a week that really put our nerves to the test.

On Wednesday and Thursday we had air raids beyond anything we had seen before, with bombs falling all around us. The one that hit nearest, not more than 30 metres away, was a huge destroyer. The detonation on impact was powerful enough to make all of us jump to our feet instantly. Just the noise of it coming in was so loud that we thought it was going to land right on top of the roof overhead. For a few very long seconds we felt like convicts facing their executioner. The old barrack we moved out of just a few days prior went kaput. The striped Lager[49] was hit by 5 bombs. The Lager for prisoners of war [POWs] got only one bomb but burned to the ground. This one was so potent that the shockwave tore out the window of our room, along with the entire frame, and swept the objects off the shelves inside. The dead bodies from the POW Lager were trucked away yesterday. It was a hill of caskets they had to move, and a sight to behold. You can imagine how we felt when, after all this, the sirens went off again

---

49 Meaning, the camp for the "stripers." Some of the prisoners in striped clothing were Hungarian Jews as well, who had been deported to Birkenau and were then selected for slave labour in Austria. Unlike Leslie's group, they worked directly under the SS, and suffered from much worse treatment.

on Friday. Luckily for us, it was just the outlying areas being bombed this time.

Now, every day, it is maddening to wait all morning until 1 o'clock [p.m.], when the raids usually cease; after that time, the planes are unlikely to come. In short, we had all been prepared to die. Then you came to visit, and along with you came renewed desire and the renewed hope that I might survive these dreadful, tempestuous times, when the smallest thing at stake is the human life, and that better days are bound to come. It was the premonition of such a better life that you brought along to our secluded barrack. I have actually dreamt of visiting you in Aspern. I wish it did not remain a dream, although I don't place much trust in it.

Father is in hospital and has probably undergone surgery on his gastric ulcer, but we do not know anything for sure about him, or he about us. It is a terrible situation to be in. Not to mention the fact that we have no stove in our room and are freezing to death. My only hope is that spring is not that far away. — This, then, is the story of how my first wish was fulfilled when I got to talk to Judit face to face. My second wish is to be freed from here.... And there are many others, more than three. Now I can hope again that all of my wishes will be fulfilled. Tomorrow I think we will have the day shift in the Neugebäude.[50]

---

50 As the buildings of the Saurerwerke had been severely damaged by the constant air raids, in February 1945 some of the machinery was evacuated to Schloss Neugebäude, a sixteenth-century castle a few kilometres to the south. Some of the Hungarian prisoners continued to work there.

To: Sarah Judith Felbermann[51]
Wien x x i. Floridsdorf
Kuenburggasse 1
Schule I. 5
From: Izrael László Frenkel
Saurer Werke Wien xi/79,
Haidestrasse 8

14.02.1945
Dear Judith,

I have been thinking about ways of promoting our reassignment to Aspern and remembered that Father, now being in hospital, could speak with Tuchmann, the hospital director.[52] He has a say in official circles and might be able to talk them into letting Saurer release us. We can probably count on him to intercede on our behalf and to tell you by letter about the result. I sent a postcard to Father telling him that what you can do on your part is to have the Aspern company put in a request for our reassignment. Get in touch by mail with Father (his address is Andor F., Spital der Israelitischen Kultusgemeinde [Hospital of the Vienna Jewish Congregation] Wien II. Malzgasse 16) telling him about the whole affair in case he has not received my card. Let him know how much you managed so far and what he is supposed to do. In any case, do visit me on Sunday if you can. Maybe we can come up with a few

---

1 This letter was postmarked on February 15, 1945, with a 6-Reichsmark stamp depicting Adolf Hitler, and it was received by Judit. According to Nazi rules, Jews were forced to add "Sarah" or "Izrael" to their names in official documents and in their correspondence so that the authorities would always know they were dealing with Jews. See page 147 for the images of these letters.
2 Dr. Emil Tuchmann (1899–1976), physician-director of the Jewish Hospital of Vienna and member of the Jewish Council.

more ideas together. By the way, we had another very bad day yester-
day. Today is better, but who knows what tomorrow will bring? Only
send notes via the hospital.

Do your best to leave no stone unturned. You might even want to
visit Father in person, as this is all very important. Greetings from all of
us, and all my best to the relatives.
  Laci

Friday, February 16 at 10:00 a.m.
My dear Judit,

I am afraid that every letter of mine starting with this one — if I can
still write at all — will be a note of farewell. All of us here in the Lager
are prepared to die any minute. I only find comfort in telling myself
that it is not going to hurt. It will take a split second, and our bodies
will be lying around scattered on the road, torn limb from limb. For
10 days now we have been living the wretched life of a convict on
death row. Our district has been showered by bombs, one for every
20 m [metres] or so. So far, I have consoled myself by the thought
that, according to the laws of probability, there was not much likeli-
hood of our shelter being hit. But by now those very laws make it
inevitable that a bomb will fall on us. This place is hell itself. Not that
the other districts have escaped the raids, but none have suffered as
badly as Simmering, and not by a small stretch. Moreover, the nar-
rower area where we live happens to be the most heavily bombed
target in Simmering. Little wonder then that I want to leave no stone
unturned in my efforts to have us transferred to another place. If anyone, only Father and you could help to get us out of here by March
1, if it's not too late by then. If everything works out, we will move to
Aspern then. But, frankly, I do not place too much trust in this. Even
if I stay alive, I will have to suffer through all the tortures of Hell.
Perhaps fate — surely a greater force than sheer good luck — will
stand by me, as it has saved me so many times before. Destiny never

deserts those it favours, not for a minute. Either way, I shall never forget the horrors of war. In some places, the front line is child's play compared to our site. Out there, an acreage as small as ours never gets hit this hard.

As to the rest, I am writing at this unusual time of the day only because yesterday I came home with a bad laryngitis and a temperature of 39°C. I stayed home for the night, so I am awake now. Going down to that damp, cold cellar with a fever is only adding injury to woe. Happily, though, the weather all through February has been as mild as if it were April. The sun is shining beautifully, and there is just a soft breeze. As nature is awakening, we are getting ready to die. But to return to the particulars: The factory was hit by 5 bombs yesterday (give or take a few), but the *Abteilung* [department] we work in is up and running. The small division assigned to the Neugebäude reported to work today as well, after being off for 3 days. Yesterday I sent a postcard to Father and Judit each, asking them to take steps toward our transfer. I will now stop writing. It's 11:00 and we must get ready for the alert. The water tower has suffered a bomb hit, so all of Vienna will have to go without water for 14 days. How are we going to wash?

In case we see each other no more, remember me fondly in your thoughts, dear Judit!

To: Mr. Andor Frenkel
Wien
16.02.1945

Dear Uncle Frenkel,

Last week my mother and I went out to the Saurer factory and agreed with the family to file a petition for them to be reassigned, first here and then to the farmlands. Unfortunately, however, I have lost the slip of paper with the dates of birth. Please be so kind as to write me these dates accurately again so that I can file the petition. And please forward

the letter to Gazsi; this would be very important. I have heard that Uncle Frenkel has been in surgery. How are you holding up? Wishing you good health, with many greetings,
Judith Felberman

The [birth] *dates (for all four of them)* [should be] *sent to József Auspitz, who delivers my letter, because as far as I understand no one can enter the hospital ...*

18.02.1945
Dear Gazsi,

Yesterday I sent a letter to your father in hospital explaining that you should file a petition for your reassignment here. Let me correct myself. Do not submit anything, in fact don't do anything in this matter. I have talked to someone in the office. He told me that Jews were not allowed to petition for anything, but that he was going to ask the Lagerführer [camp leader], *who is known to be amenable to such requests. If the Lagerführer requests or actually demands your reassignment, you will have to be released without any strings attached. The only thing that matters is that you should be registered to the city, as I am. Unfortunately, it is a rather lengthy procedure before this can be settled.*

There have been several times this week when I could have gone to see you if the streetcars were running. I cannot possibly undertake such a long journey on foot, much as I would like to see you. But as soon as the streetcar service resumes, hopefully in a day or two, I will be able to go. I would prefer to go during the week rather than on Sunday. The last time we went out they made a big fuss about it. Detectives, bicycle police, and closed gates everywhere. I do not like this. And to you it makes no difference, since you are always there during the day anyway. But I am restless to go. Since I went to visit you and saw the circumstances there, I haven't had a moment's peace of mind. I am not worried about myself; I only pray that they [the bombs] *keep out of that place. After each air raid I want to rush, to fly there, or at least to find out, by telephone or* [somehow] *else, if you are all right. Alas, this is impossible. That leaves us with corresponding more frequently, writing to each other at least every other day. Just a few words, if nothing else, to say we are fine, we are alive. If you send a postcard, I'll get that, too.*

On Monday I will find out how it went with the Lagerführer. If I don't get to see you till then, I will write right away.

Until then, many greetings,

Judit

P.S. Even though you need not file a petition, it is useful for you to know that we have told them [the authorities] *that your father is Mom's stepbrother, being the son of my grandmother's first husband. The truth is that my grandmother never remarried, and my mother never had a stepbrother, but they do not need to know that.*

To: Mr. Andor Frenkel
Malzgasse, Wien
From: Judith Felberman

21.02.1945
Dear Uncle Frenkel,

I believe Laci has informed you, and I have also told you by mail, that we are doing our best to have us reassigned to the Floridsdorf Lager. Once there, if possible, we would report for farmland work. Sarkadi will speak with the Lagerführer here tomorrow, introducing himself as Jóska Grosz. Géza Lieberman and the superiors at Aspern have advised us to speak with Tuchmann, the head surgeon of the hospital, because he has the most say, and if there is anything to be done at all, he is the one with the means to do it. I don't know what terms you are on with him but do talk to him by all means and ask him to do everything in his power to have the Saurer release the family as superfluous labour force, to be reassigned here. There may be another way as well, but he will know it better. And please make sure to keep me informed about the developments.

Wishing you speedy recovery, with many greetings,

Judith Felberman

22.02.1945

Dear Gazsi,

I don't know if you got the letter I addressed to your father, so I am writing again. Unfortunately, I am unable to see you in person, as the streetcars are not in service. We have talked to our Lagerführer, who agreed to admit you all if the authorities over there approve your release. The procedure would look like this: Your superior (labour supervisor or foreman) in charge of managing your affairs writes a letter to the Lagerführer here, explaining that your relatives are over there in Floridsdorf, and you would like to join them. He should state that he consents to your reassignment and ask the Lagerführer if he has any objection. If he has none, he will write an approval clause on the letter. His address is:

An die Lagerleitung der Lager K.21 Kuenburg [gasse],

zu Händen des Herrn [to the attention of] *Lagerführer Josef Simonovitz*[53]

This is the first and most important step. Next, he returns the signed letter to you. You forward it to the Sonderkommando[54] *enclosing a petition of a few lines in which you provide your years of birth and ask your request for reassignment to the Floridsdorf Lager to be granted on the grounds that it has already been approved by both parties.*

---

53 A camp maintained by the City of Vienna in District XXI, 1 Kuenburggasse, in a former school. See the introduction for further information.

54 German; special command: the SS unit overseeing the camps.

The sooner you take care of this the better, because our reassignment to Aspern is around the corner. True enough, I have no idea if we have a chance to make it there at all, as they require 80 individuals <u>fit for work</u>,[55] and we have our grandmother [with us] who is incapacitated. But for now nothing is certain, as far as I know. But even if we must remain here, Floridsdorf is still better than Simmering.

Many greetings until I see you again,

Judith

Thursday, February 22 at 10:00 a.m.

My dear Judit,

Since February 7, we have had no more than 3 days without an alert. Those were the days when Judit and company were visiting. On all other days, sometime between 11:00 and 12:00 a kid calls out the cue words "Steiermark, Carinthia,"[56] prompting us to get dressed. Then soon the kukukk [the signal] is sounded, followed by the *Werksalarm* [factory alarm] and finally the siren alert, and we start marching toward the shelter, which is quite a distance away. This is the order of the day. It was the routine yesterday, the day before yesterday, and it will be the same today and tomorrow — if we live to see it, that is. And so far it's been during the day only. Now they [the Allied planes] are going to fly over during the night, too. Twice a day. Not that it matters whether we are to die in darkness or broad daylight, but packing your bag is much more of a nuisance at night.

A Jewish teaching tells us to repent one day before we die.[57] What this really means is that we need to repent each day, because it is

---

55 Underlined in the original.

56 A reference to the two Austrian provinces Allied planes crossed before reaching Lower Austria (Vienna).

57 A reference to Rabbi Eliezer's teaching in Pirkei Avot 2:15 (Ethics of the Fathers), a section of the Mishnah.

always possible that we will die the next. This doctrine has become obsolete in these times, when no one can vouch for our lives thirty minutes down the line. These days, we should repent every waking minute. It's gotten to the point when I no longer even feel like reporting on the air raids. It has become such an overdone topic. By contrast, the fear of death itself, the feeling you get in your stomach as the planes fly over and bombs zip through the air, always strikes you with the force of novelty, no matter how many times you have felt it before. Every time the aircraft make their approach, I think *this is it*, this must be the wave bringing my death to me. This possibility is maintained until the alert is called off, ushering in a few hours of respite and peace, perhaps. So it is hardly surprising that I keep harping about the raids after all, but this is our life here and now. Unpack, pack again, to the shelter again. If only I could move to another Lager!

Today Nusi suffered some kind of injury at the factory so she went into the hospital to be tested for internal bleeding, I believe. I sent another letter to Father with her, asking him to plead our case for transfer. *Dum spiro spero.* [While I breathe, I hope.] Elsewhere there is nothing new. I stayed at home another night yesterday instead of picking up my shift at the factory. After a stint in the shelter, I regularly measure my temperature at 37.7°C still. This was the seventh night in a row I was able to sleep through. And what a fine thing that is! It's only when you are sick that you realize how precious health is; you need to be orphaned before you realize what a mother means; and you must work the night shift to truly appreciate a good night's sleep.

May God be with you!

Monday, February 26 at 16:00 [4:00 p.m.]
My dear Judit,

It ain't over till it's over, as they say. Even though the sun has not set quite yet, I believe we got away with [survival] for the day. Just an hour ago the *Voralarm* [pre-alarm] was sounded, but they called it off. If the planes are not coming at the usual time, they won't be coming on a given day. We are toughing it out one day at a time, sighing in relief every time the danger zone of the day is past, and beginning to hope that we shall be spared until the next afternoon.

This month of February has been long beyond words, and it's not even over yet. The bombing raids only began on the 7th, but the 20 days since have seemed an eternity, filled with a sense of being on the brink of annihilation. Since Thursday the week before last I haven't been to the factory, but today I am feeling better, so I will have to report for work. That's quite all right, as I have been sleeping long and well these past 11 days, staying in. I think I will get the daytime shift next week anyway, although there is a chance that the work in the Neugebäude will be prolonged for a few more weeks. I believe my heart has had some much-needed rest. True enough, I have lost quite a bit of weight during my illness, as I had no appetite to eat anything other than a bowl of soup here and there.

These days Mom has a daily job peeling potatoes, leaving me and Gyuri to take care of most household chores. We still haven't heard anything about Father. Some people may go to the hospital tomorrow, and then we will find out.

As for our transfer I petitioned, I have lost all hope. If we haven't received notice thus far, nothing is going to happen until Thursday. At least you could have come to visit one more time, my Judit! I wouldn't have wished for anything else if you had. But that last, unexpected visit of yours, when you showed up like a comet, was followed by deadly silence. I haven't heard from you or about you since that day. And to think that in a few days you will have moved to Aspern, far from the maddening world of air raids! I wish to God I could turn back the wheel of time to that day on July 1 and miraculously change everything that came after. If I could, my mother and father would not have succumbed to disease, nor would I look the way I do today. Even so, I'd have nothing to complain about if only I could be sure that we will eventually make it home safe and sound. War is war, and if we manage to live through this, we will be able to make a new start, and I may yet hope to pursue my chosen profession. May destiny bring us together again, my Judit!

Bye

Monday, March 5 at 9:00 a.m.
My dear Judit,

I should have written sooner, but this week I resumed my job at the factory and didn't have the time. First and foremost, I must record that Judit and her mother paid another visit on Wednesday. They went through fire and brimstone and finally managed to persuade their *Lagerführer* to admit us pending our release by Saurer. So the thing left to arrange is to have them approve our transfer on this side. On Friday some people from here went to the hospital. I sent with them a letter to Father, updating him on the whole affair. I told him we should have Tuchmann intercede, because even if we secured approval of our transfer relocation to Floridsdorf, it is far from certain they will put in a claim for us to move on to Aspern. Indeed, our transfer directly to Aspern should be the first priority. Father wrote back to say he was so sick he was unable to speak with Tuchmann or to help us with the case in any other way. So at this point it looks like the transfer claim will take months to be heard unless someone at the Sonder[58] agrees to further our cause. By then, our loved ones will have left Aspern, and we will be stuck in Floridsdorf — from the frying pan into the fire, as it were. The way to do it should be to have Judit take care of our transfer directly to Aspern. When that is done, Father may be well enough to do his part.

As to his condition, he says in his letter that he felt very weak for 10 days, but on the 11th day, just as he was getting better, his ulcer

---

58 See the footnote to the letter of February 22.

began to fester. Since then they have been cleaning it every day. It must be a rather painful procedure. Father says it's not that big a deal, just sheer bad luck, in that it will prolong his hospitalization by 4 weeks. That's quite a long time. Certainly long enough for us all to stay alive. I would very much like to see him here, to hear his voice, to have him tell us all about what happened at the hospital. Alas, that possibility seems very remote. If only I could visit him myself! Fortunately, Judit and her family are allowed to visit him and to keep in touch with me. In this way I can see him and her in my mind, if not in the flesh. At least this connects me somewhat to life, to the world outside, and gives me hope that one day I will get to see the sun instead of living only in the dark. Your visit, my Judit, is like visiting someone on his deathbed, breathing some life back into him. When you come, I am renewed in my hope that I will have a wonderful life one day. I used to count the weeks, then just the months. Shall I say we have entered the ninth month? I only wish for this labour not to go post-term! May that child be born at the end of the ninth month, to the day. My Judit, I can hardly wait for your next visit. I wish I could go to see you myself!

Bye, my Judit!

Monday, March 12 at 9:00 a.m.
My dear Judit,

This is to thank you for your visit yesterday. When you are all here, I must act in such an aloof, ordinary way with you, without so much as uttering a word of heartfelt intimacy, lest people in the barrack start gossiping about how we were drooling all over each other. But what I set on paper here will never be read by anyone but you. I have decided to show you these pages if you come down next Sunday. Nobody else will need to know. I believe this diary will reveal the extent of my love for you plainly. True enough, your demonstration of love through action [by her visit] is worth a thousand pages. I wish I had the means to manifest my own love in that way. But unfortunately, it's the circumstances that determine one's actions. Perhaps one day I will have the opportunity to show you that my love for you doesn't stop at mere words but can be proven through deeds.

You said you might be leaving your Lager soon. Where to, no one knows, but presumably it will be to Germany. You kept reminding me that this last visit of yours could well be one of farewell. I cannot believe, and will not believe, that you should be wrenched from me so soon after we first met. But here we have living proof that we are too strong to be separated, that we shall find each other sooner or later, even if we must go to the other side of the world. Our fate, our destiny, is that we both must suffer in the present, so that we may be happy together in the future. How long the story of such a great love as ours can be! And it's all so much easier to bear if we are in it together, even if in physical separation that prevents us from seeing each other except on the rare occasion. When you leave, a part of you will stay here with me. You will come to me every day, and our conversation will be much more open and intimate than when you were here in person, because these imaginary meetings won't be disturbed by uninvited guests. And I shall be with you on your way, never deserting you, always keeping you from harm. You must not be hurt, because you belong to me! And when we meet again, as we certainly shall, my dear Judit, trust me that the whole world will be lying at our feet! You said the sick had already left your Lager, and the rest had been conscripted as well. So it looks like all of you will be gone before long, despite some inevitable delay. Things happen faster over there because your Lager is a big one, but it will be followed by the lesser ones, including ours, at a later date.

The news here is that, as far as I know, I will be working the day shift this week. Father is feeling better. Mom works every other day peeling potatoes, and Gyuri has been on the day shift for a week now.

Sunday, March 18 at 10:30 a.m.

My dear Judit,

This week I got my workload all right. I am not sure if it means good fortune or bad luck, but I am assigned to the night shift at the Neugebäude starting Tuesday. It's a bad deal because the Neuge is 3 or 4 km [kilometres] away, so we need to get going earlier and get home later, accounting for the half-hour commute each way. But it's a good deal because it leaves us entirely free.

Let me explain how a typical night goes. At a quarter past seven in the evening, we leave the barrack. It's just the three of us, Mrs. Huber, Ilonka [Lili] Nasch and me, without any *Werkschutz*. We wait for the striped convoy to pass to the front, as they have the flashlights. Without them, we wouldn't see the huge bomb craters in the road. We get to the site at 8:00 and rest in the office until about 9:00. Then we go upstairs and work all night, taking turns every 4 hours or so. That's enough time for me to get all the required work done if I do it fast, so I get to spend the rest of the night (about 5 hours) sleeping. At 6:00 we leave for the barrack. (We can come to the site earlier if we like. Here, we can do as we please all night long.) We have no *Werkschutz* accompanying us on the way back, either; in fact, we wouldn't have any even if we asked for it. Upstairs we get no inspectors, no visitors of any kind all night, so we can sit down, sleep or work as we see fit. On the way there and back we are free to choose our own route and pace, moving as fast or as slowly as we want (if you can call that a degree of freedom). So we get home in the morning almost fully rested, and the little additional sleep before noon makes it complete. I think I got the better end of the deal after all. The only hitch is that there is no rotation, so I will have to stay on the night shift until things have settled. Then we will be working the day shift until further notice. Do come over this afternoon, my dear. I can hardly wait to see you!

Monday, March 19 at 5:30 p.m.
My dear Judit,

I am remembering that unforgettable day of March 19, 1944. We went by Peti's place and learned that the railway stations in Pest [Budapest] had been occupied by the troops of the Reich. Then we left to continue our walk outside. By then, my friendship with you had grown profound and genuine. I did not have a care for anything but you and my studies. At the time, I had no idea that this date would be etched in my mind forever. The year since then has been a long one, but our love has stood the test by fire, perhaps more steadfastly than if we had stayed together. I am proud of my love for you and of your fidelity to me through this year of our hardship. The only thing that worries me now is that you never came to visit yesterday. There was a massive air raid in Floridsdorf on Friday... Or have you left the Lager already? Or was it just the *Voralarm* preventing you? I don't know what to think. I am desperate to hear from you. Tonight we are going to work at 7:00, earlier than usual, and we will have Saturday night off.

To: Mr. László Frenkel
Wien II.
Malzgasse 7

20.03.1945
Dear Gazsi,

I apologize for not having made good on my promise to visit you on Sunday, but the streetcar rails and wires are so badly damaged around here, and I would think in your area too, that this would have been quite impossible. I did want to say goodbye to you before we leave Vienna. For we are going to move on; it has been settled. The last I have heard is that we are setting out sometime tomorrow during the morning hours, but we don't know where to. We only assume it will be via

Strasshof to Theresienstadt[59] *near Prague.*Ƴ [marking in original] *I wouldn't mind if we could be sure about this, as I have heard very nice things about it. Best of all, there are no air raids there. It would be so nice to move to a place like this after Floridsdorf. What happened here last week is not something we could endure for long. I don't know if you have heard, but we were literally bombed out. The entire school building burned down, and we lost many of our belongings in the fire. Luckily, we had been ushered to the underground shelter, although those who stayed behind escaped unhurt as well, except for the four or five who died inside the building. I did not know any of them. Now we are put up in the other school, crammed together with those already there. All 74 of us in a single room, crouching, lying down or kneeling on the floor as best as we can, unable to sleep for the fleas. I don't think it can get any worse than this. But the worst pain is to know that we won't be able to see each other again for a while if we leave here. It was better, after all, while I could go to see you once in a while. Even as I write this I don't know what is happening with you. How can you be so cruel as to not send a few words after such a terrible week? At least it was terrible for us, to be sure; I don't know if you had such massive air raids over there.*

I will send a postcard to the hospital directly before our departure. And I will write to you on the way, except that I have very few cards left, and I cannot buy more as they have run out.

By way of farewell I wish you all good luck and happiness with all

---

59 Theresienstadt was a Nazi ghetto and concentration camp established in 1941 at the site of a former Austro-Hungarian garrison town (Terezín, Czech Republic today). In the final phase of the war, several transports of Hungarian Jewish prisoners ended up there. The Theresienstadt ghetto also served propaganda purposes and functioned to camouflage the deprivations prisoners experienced there. In the early summer of 1944, the prisoners' living conditions and camp facilities were improved in order to misguide the representatives of the Red Cross who visited the site. This is probably why Judit refers to hearing "very nice things about it."

my heart. I hope to see you before we can all go home, or else at a pleas-
ant, peaceful place somewhere back home. And you know where that
place is.

 Until then, many greetings to all in the family, and especially to you,
Judith

♈ *We get this hint as the first transport was dispatched there. People in*
our Lager have already received letters from them.

Monday, March 26 at 4:00 p.m.
My dear, dear, dear Judit,

Two weeks ago, during your last visit, you said you had all come to
say goodbye. I didn't believe a word of it at the time. I was sure they
were not going to take you away as yet. But on Saturday I learned that
everyone in your Lager had packed and gone. You can imagine how
I was affected by the news. When you left after your visit last time, I
regretted not having shown you this diary. Now you may never get
to read these lines addressed to you. Until now I was at least reas-
sured to know that you were near me, in Vienna, and that we had the
means to keep in touch, by correspondence if nothing else. Now I
have no idea which corner of the world you have moved to, for better
or worse. Will we meet again in this life? Or have we been completely
torn apart by this formidable conflagration? In any case, I'm writing
down once again what is already so obvious: I love you as I have never
loved a girl before, and I shall never forget you, who sweetened my
bitter captivity. From the time we found ourselves in the ghetto (not
to mention before that date) to this very day, you have been the one
whose very thought instantly made even the worst torment easier to
suffer. We had not been together very long, and it is possible that my
overheated love for you is not being fuelled by your person so much
as by the extraordinary times we live in.

 Admittedly, I am struggling to find the words that could convey

what you mean to me — perhaps not less than my mother, a source
of nourishment to fall back upon. Whenever I felt dejected, I always
told myself that I only needed to hold out until you and I could re-
unite, and I shall be rewarded by happiness. I count the few times you
came out to visit among the finest days of my life, except that all that
joy prevented me from exploiting them to the full. In my incapac-
ity I was reminded of how Petőfi felt in his poem *Plans Gone Up in
Smoke*.[60] I just kept looking at you, listening to your voice, without
even saying I love you, but you must have seen that love in my eyes,
just as I was fully conscious of your love for me emanating from your
whole being. Once I wrote in my diary that the more one expends on
the other — more time, more thought, more deeds — the more that
other is being loved. Giving is actually better than receiving at growing love. You have lavished much of your time and energy on me. I
needed every ounce of love I could get. And if I didn't love you for
the profuse love I received from you, then I love you for how much
I have given you — for the days of dreaming about you, the minutes
spent thinking about you, for this diary here, and everything else I
have offered to you. But whatever I have received from you I could
only repay by my own self. I hope you will get your reward one day.

Bye, bye, bye, my dear! I shall see you soon.

Tuesday, March 27 at 3:00 p.m.
My Darling,

People who went into the hospital from here returned with the news
that those in Floridsdorf were gone. And I got this letter from you,
dated the 20th this month, in which you say it is more than like-

---

60 A poem by the well-known Hungarian poet Sándor Petőfi (*Füstbe ment terv*,
1844): "I leapt into the tiny room/ She ran, she flew to me/ I clung to her without
a word/ Like fruit clings to the tree." English translation by Leslie A. Kery.

ly that you will be leaving the following morning. This means you were probably gone by the 21st. You also let me know you have gone through a series of terrible raids in recent weeks. Your Lager was all bombed out but none of you got hurt. (And you won't, because you belong to me.) You say you are probably going to Theresienstadt near Prague, as the previous convoys (and, as I understand today, the ones after you) have all ended up there.[61] You are happy about it, because at least there are no air raids there. I wish I could be there with you! As you boarded the cattle car, did you think of that other journey by rail, which you and I had shared together? I can imagine how miserable you must have felt having to travel without me this time. All you had to keep you company on this present journey were your memories.

Even as I write these lines you may be in Prague thinking of me and of Vienna, where you spent nearly nine months of your life. And if you are, I am sure you feel just as sad as I do, no matter how much better off you are in that new place. Now that we have been separated, captivity tastes entirely different to me. Not waiting for your next letter, for you to show up on Sundays anymore, makes it all the more austere. But at least now I no longer have to worry about you having been hurt every time another air raid comes around. I hope your life has taken a turn for the better, if only so that the next time we meet you may look just as beautiful, rosy-cheeked and voluptuous as when you left. For you struck me as extremely attractive then, you see.

Father has written to tell me he is feeling better. He is still not much to look at, but he is able to take food now and is slowly regaining his strength. His general mood is hopeful. I so want him to be with us already!

---

61 In fact, Judit's group — unlike four thousand other Hungarian prisoners — never left for Theresienstadt because on March 26 a huge air raid destroyed the Strasshof railway station, making further transports impossible. (Lappin-Eppel, *Deportations of Hungarian Jews to Austria*, 73).

I have no new details to report. This week I have the night shift again in the Neugebäude, but the week is only 5 days long. Last night I slept for 7 hours. I feel so rested that I wouldn't be able to go to sleep even if I wanted to. I spent the morning reading, and the afternoon so far (it's around half past three) writing and getting some cooking done in between. Now I am going to wash my hair, then study some math and German. The rest looks like this: getting up at a quarter to 6:00, leaving just after quarter past 6:00, picking up the shift at 7:00, going to sleep at 9:00, and sleeping till half past three in the morning. This is my foreseeable schedule, then. Oh, and we didn't have an air-raid alert today, for the first time in I don't know how many weeks. — My Judit, we shall stay together come what may, shall we not?

Monday, April 2 at 9:00 a.m.
My Judit,

We are seeing fateful days. The front line is inching closer and closer. Now we can hear shots being fired here and there, and the horizon is tinged red at noon. Everyone is agitated, and there is tension in the air. The *Ausländers* [foreigners] are being rounded up and marched away to dig trenches. The sky is teeming with Russian aircraft almost all the time, dropping bombs everywhere. We do not even have air-raid alerts anymore.

III. 27. kedd

(50)

Drágám!

du 15 óra

[handwritten diary entry in Hungarian]

IV. 2. hétfő

Drága Andikám!

de 9 óra

[handwritten diary entry in Hungarian]

The last two entries in Leslie's diary, March 27 and April 2, 1945.

Memoir

In memoriam of my brother, George (1929–1955).

Author's Preface

My diary of our Lager life now strikes me as unbelievably naive. When I wrote it, I didn't know what was happening in other camps, what life was like in other parts of Europe or about the terrible fate of the six million European Jews who would be killed. I was absolutely convinced that we were in a very bad situation. It was not true. We received special treatment in the factory where we worked, in the Lager where we stayed for about nine months and in the city of Vienna, where we were allowed to move freely toward the end of our captivity when we had to walk to the factory, which was far from the Lager.

Aside from being ignorant and naive, I was also nineteen years old, with all the implications of this age: I was full of sentimentality, excitement and enthusiastic expectations concerning my future after the war. I didn't doubt for a moment that we would eventually be liberated from our precarious situation.

Finally, there was my sweetheart whom I loved and with whom I arranged a regular correspondence, which occupied our lives and kept our spirits high in the most difficult days of our captivity.

My diary contains discrepancies in the ways it describes the food, the difficulties, the night shift, my relationship with other people. In the months during which I wrote the diary many things changed — just as I did. I always wrote what I felt at any particular moment, independently of what I might have written a few days earlier. My sincerity took precedence over consistency.

We knew that we were living in the last phase of the war and that our survival would be the beginning of a new life. That, alongside my optimism, explains why I felt it was so important to study even in the Lager: I was preparing myself for the future.

In retrospect I find that, in spite of the constant dangers and insecurity, one can find very little reference to God in my diary. Sometimes I relate to the Roman goddess Fortuna, or to Fate or to the sheer luck that protected me in those difficult times. It was difficult to trust in God when He had abandoned us and pushed us away. *Eli, Eli, lama sabachtani?* (My God, my God, why hast Thou forsaken me?)[1] How sad and tragic it is that this Evil wasn't satisfied that it took away our liberty, took our loved ones and our lives. It also took away our God, our faith and all the spiritual values that kept us through the millennia.

---

1   Matthew 27:46, based on Psalm 22:2.

The Streets of My Childhood

As I remember and reconstruct the memories that have been stored in the crevices of my brain, I realize that some events may not have happened exactly the same way as I remember them. As time passes, colour and light change, backgrounds widen or narrow, objects and people either assume new importance or disappear in the dark shadows. It is as though my past assumes a new life.

But the deeper my memories lurk, the more fascinating the past is for me. Small events come back and evoke odd feelings, sitting in my memory and becoming part of me. I cannot toss them out of my mind, so I write them down. This way, I expose them, and so they become a reality. They will play themselves out again and again and when they are read, the stories will become part of my history.

The first memories of my life are connected with homes, the anchors of childhood. My earliest recollection takes me back to my first home in Debrecen, Hungary, on Darabos Street (Rothermere Street, at the time). I see a vision of my mother and me in our little house looking out of the window, watching the children playing on the street. I was born in 1925 and would have been about three years old then; my mother, Flora, thirty-two. The magic of reimagining the past makes me see the outside of the house as well, which would have been seen only by the two or three children, their clothing worn and creased, who were playing outside. The children were noisy, their play full of movement and laughter. I assume they didn't wear shoes. Shoes do not fit into this picture.[1]

By the fourth year of their marriage, my parents could not afford to stay in an expensive part of the city.[2] At that time, my father, Andor, was a partner in a grain business with a relative. Later they split, probably because the business did not go well. I didn't hear too much about this enterprise because of that. My father later went into partnership with his brother-in-law, my uncle Zoli Kovács. They had two leather stores in Debrecen — one which my father managed and one which my uncle managed, and both of which they had to give up at the end of 1943 because of the restrictive anti-Jewish laws, which prohibited Jewish merchants from having access to the official leather supply.[3]

Through my uncle's connections and by means of illegal manoeuvrings, he managed to get hold of some leather. By the time the authorities found out about these illegal transactions and wanted to question him, he had managed to get himself a passport and had left for British Mandate Palestine. His family had to stay behind, though, and as my uncle had entrusted his family's care to my father, our two families moved in together. From that time on, my father had to work

---

1   Even before the Great Depression many Hungarians lived on the margins. It was not unusual for poor working-class children to run around barefoot.

2   The most fashionable parts of Debrecen included the modern high-quality apartment buildings with full-comfort homes erected in the main streets and squares. Darabos Street, with its one-storey houses with gardens mostly built in the late nineteenth and early twentieth century, can be categorized as a modest middle-class neighbourhood.

3   According to the Second "Jewish Law" (Act IV of 1939), no trade licence to sell goods under state monopoly was to be issued to Jews. Due to the gradually increasing shortage of raw material after Hungary had entered the war, only vendors appointed by the state were allowed to trade leather, and therefore Jews had been excluded from this business by 1943.

three times as hard to provide a living for all of us. When all the leather supplies dried up, my father opened a fine-leather goods store.

My father kept the books for the business. He had graduated from a school of commerce and knew bookkeeping. In the evenings, he would enter the items in a large ledger in even, small, rounded letters. I think it was my uncle who had made the business decisions, but my father, a quiet, mild-mannered man, didn't really mind. After he closed the store at six o'clock in the evening, he would live only for his family. At home, he listened to the radio, read the paper and spent time with us. He was fond of playing chess, and when I was fighting with my younger brother by four years, Gyuri (George) — which happened sometimes — he tried to dispense justice to us. He liked to go to bed early because he always woke up early in the morning and wasn't able to get back to sleep. At 6:00 a.m., in both winter and summer, he would bike over to the swimming pool in the Nagyerdő, the Great Forest, a large park where he would exercise and socialize. Other than that, my parents didn't have many friends outside of our family. On Friday evenings, we would visit my aunt Irén's family after supper, and sometimes Mother's cousin Gizi would come to our place. I don't recall any other visitors or guests. Maybe every now and then some relative from the countryside would show up at our home, but we had no social life in today's sense of the word.

My father wasn't a talkative man. He always had stomach problems and perhaps that's why he didn't seek out other people's company. I remember only one conversation with him from my childhood. I couldn't have been more than ten years old and the two of us were sitting on a bench in the corridor of some public office. Of the surroundings, what I can remember are white walls and the spittoons that used to be a common feature of offices in those days. While we were waiting for our turn, my father was talking to me about liberalism. He spoke in a calm voice but with great enthusiasm. I don't recall the exact words, only the content of his speech. According to my father, liberalism meant freedom from all forms of oppression.[4] That conversation left a deep imprint on me — after all, I still retain the memory. It filled me with pride that he shared his thoughts with me. Later on, when I was already a "big boy," I was often surprised to notice that when I advanced my opinion on some subject, my father would listen with evident interest.

My mother, too, lived only for us — my father, me and Gyuri. Her main daily preoccupation was what to cook for lunch the next day and making sure that everyone would be happy with the dishes she prepared. From morning until noon, she was busy cooking with the housemaid. After the midday meal, she would have a little rest, after which we would go to the promenade on Piac Street, the main street of Debrecen, for a stroll. She'd spend her evenings mending our socks, doing some sewing or reading. She would always be reading books while our father was reading the newspaper. I read both.

From Darabos Street we moved to Csapó Street, one of the main streets to shop in Debrecen. My father's store was on the same street, so he didn't have too far to go to get to work. There were two separate yards for the house — the front one belonged to the landlord, and the one in the back, surrounded by a wire fence, was where we had our home. The fence was probably the most appealing feature of the place when my father rented the apartment because it kept me within limits. Old, huge trees were in front of the house and a swing hung from a branch of one of the trees. When my cousin Imre from Török-szentmiklós was our summer guest we played a lot with the swing. I recall some words from my cousin's favourite song as, "Adieu my little dear, brave lieutenant…"[5] The lyrics still have a strong effect on me,

---

4   Note that the ideology of the regime in which Leslie grew up was built upon anti-socialist and anti-liberal ideas. In the popular discourse of the era, "liberalism" was often used as a swear word.

5   The song "Adieu, My Little Guard Lieutenant" originates from the 1908 operetta of the Austrian composer Robert Stolz, *Die lustigen Weiber von Wien* (*The Merry Wives of Vienna*).

perhaps because I heard them so long ago. The song evoked smiling, waving soldiers looking out of the window of a military train going to World War I and happy, proud people standing on the station platform waving back. Later on, when I lived through the war in my own lifetime, the image had a different association for me.

From a young age, my father made me take violin lessons. My first teacher's method was a bit eccentric: after a brief introduction to the basics, I had to play pieces from music sheets that he transcribed himself. Later, my father decided that I should continue my studies in a music school. There, they came to the conclusion that it would be best if I forgot everything I had previously learned and start my violin studies all over again! I was also taught music theory on Saturday afternoons, and though I had to attend those classes, I was excused from writing because on the Sabbath I was not supposed to write.

I always liked music but was not that fond of playing the violin. More precisely, I didn't like to practise. The daily hour of practice would only occur after much pleading and threatening on my mother's part, and if I managed to skim ten minutes off the hour, I was happy. After many years of studying, we stopped the violin lessons, partly because I got fed up with practising and partly because my mother got fed up with having to beg me all the time. I haven't held a violin in my hands since then, yet I really like music — especially violin pieces.

From Csapó Street, we moved to 11 Széchenyi Street, which was closer to my school.[6] I was six years old when we moved, and we lived there for almost seven years. Whenever I remember my early childhood, my thoughts bring me back here. I can still clearly envision the furnishings of our home, which contained three spacious rooms, a kitchen and a bathroom. There was a pantry as well, with a

---

6   The Jewish Grammar School of Debrecen on Simonffy Street.

blue lard-holder and lots of fruit jars full of homemade preserves, the pride of my mother. In the kitchen stood a black wood-fire stove, a wooden table with two square stools and, in the small anteroom that separated the kitchen from the rest of the house, a white chest.

In this white chest I collected the first page of the daily newspaper — in a way, collecting history. When I was six or seven years old, I received my own "newspaper" every Saturday morning, a very highly anticipated newspaper, *Az Én Ujságom*, that was only for children. I always read it from cover to cover. In the summertime, when this anteroom was full of sunshine, my mother would bring out a little wheeled table tied to a little chair. On the table a soft-boiled egg was poured into the middle of a mashed-potato ring — my favourite food.

In the middle of our living room stood a square dining table with four chairs. In the summer the room would shine, and the fine food would smell delicious. On winter afternoons, when darkness descended, we would pull the table close to the window, take off its cover and my little brother and I would do our homework. The other part of the room would already be in semi-darkness when it was still too early to turn on the light. The tile stove that stood at the far corner of the room radiated pleasant warmth. The atmosphere was warm all around, and the silence was broken only by deep sighs indicating that either a task was finally done or a serious problem had yet to be overcome.

The next room was the dining room. In the middle was a big oval dining table that was rarely used. It was set perhaps on High Holy Days, but I don't remember even one occasion when a dinner party was given in this room. The table was covered by a nice multi-coloured Gobelin tablecloth, which was my mother's handiwork. Two credenzas contained the necessary plates and cutlery, the ones that were probably never used.

With noisy, always moving, quarrelling kids, constantly working, cooking, cleaning women, sounds of the radio, talking and music whirling, this was an active, busy household. Motion was everywhere — from the kitchen in the morning to learning and playing in the afternoon to preparation for the evening in the bedroom.

Except the dining room. It stood in its quiet loneliness. Not participating in anything, not offering any use. The chairs not to sit on, the table not to eat on or even to use for school purposes. But it made the home elegant, spacious, good to look at. From here one door opened to the living room and one to the bedroom, where my parents slept on a double bed and George on a couch. I occupied the other couch in the living room. In the summertime both doors were always open and together the three rooms presented a pleasant sight.

The reason we had moved, as I mentioned, was to be closer to the school, which was right behind our house on a street that ran parallel. On the first day of school my mother came with me, showing me the way by crossing a large yard, but coming home I was alone. I think we finished the day earlier than planned because my mother was a bit surprised when I showed up at the door. From then on, I always went to school alone.

The first-class teacher was Aunt Ilonka.[7] She was a plain-faced and slim-shaped woman, and I still have two memories going back to her, after almost ninety years. One is of having to go to a medical inspection with my class, where everybody had to undress, and of feeling a bit disturbed to be naked in her presence. The other recollection I have is of her praising me when I could read Hebrew fluently.

From the second year on, the principal taught us. He was the husband of Aunt Ilonka and was as homely as his wife but much shorter. He treated the rich and the poor children differently. If the

Aunt Ilonka is not a biological relation. In Hungarian the word *néni* (aunt/auntie) is often used as a term of respect or affection for an older person; *bácsi* (uncle) is the male equivalent.

poor children didn't behave well they got heck, but the rich children escaped with a verbal reprimand. I was in the category of the latter group because I took German lessons he taught after-hours. When the course was over, I could read and write the language well.

In the second class, math was a serious subject. We had to count till one hundred, and we had to know the multiplication table. The principal was our teacher up till the fourth class and he sent us over to high school with good mathematical knowledge.

When we were in third class, we could borrow books from the school library. I still remember the title of the first book I took out! It was *Three Boy Scouts in Africa*. It was summertime, and when I went home with the book the living room was cool and pleasant. The couch was tempting and I lay down and started to read, feeling like a very mature boy.

Even in elementary school, parents were always invited to the closing ceremonies at the end of each school year. On one of those occasions I sang in the choir as my mother sat in the first row in front of us. Later, when we were at home, I turned to my mother and told her, "Mommy, I looked at all the mothers in the audience and I have to tell you that you were the most beautiful of all of them."

On this day, she must have been the happiest mother in the whole world.

On a sunny morning in June, we were coming home from another closing ceremony, my mother and me. A big bouquet was in my hand. Everything was radiant, gloriously shining around us. The school year was finished. Here was the long-awaited vacation, promising a happy summer, three months of fun. It was June of 1933. At that time Hitler was already in power.

~

Another feature of Széchenyi Street was the big market that was set up every spring and autumn and ran from our house to the end of the street. On long afternoons I liked strolling among the colourful tents, stopping at every stand to examine the goods being exhibited.

In my pocket I always had a little money and depending on my available funds and the price of the merchandise, I would buy a fountain pen or just a piece of chocolate. I liked to get lost in the crowd and walk around without any destination, just going and going. At the end of the street there was a carousel and the circus. I didn't go into the circus, but I would sit on the carousel, and in front of the circus tent I would listen to the speech of the barkers. Out would come the dwarfs, the muscle-men and other odd specimens and after the speeches, when everybody went back behind the curtains, I would walk away to see how the servant girls tried to pick up the soldiers. I was interested in everybody and everything.

Beside our house stood a large, three-storey building called the Royal Court of Justice; everyone called it the *tábla*. Its back windows opened to our yard, and we could see the prisoners cleaning the royal windows. Only once did we have a little commotion in our yard, when we learned that women who had poisoned their husbands were being transported to the building. They were simple peasant women, which surprised me. I came to realize, then, that no visible sign distinguishes an honest person from an evil criminal.

During this time, I went through the four years of elementary school and three years of junior high. Everything that was good to remember happened here at Széchenyi Street. Every summer, every winter, was a new adventure, whether watering the rose bushes or wading in the knee-high snow. It was here that I learned how to skip hopscotch; how to aim the little clay balls to win games; how to ride a bike. First, it was my father's big bicycle he taught me on, and because my legs were not long enough to reach the pedals, my father ran alongside me and held the seat. If I fell and scratched my skin, he put cigarette paper on it. Sometimes I looked like a badly rolled cigarette.

Debrecen had an area with cold and warm water pools. It opened when I was six years old and we took advantage of it early. On Sundays, the whole family rented a cabin and we spent the whole day there. Many years after that I was a member of a sports club, and in the early mornings I was in regular training there. I participated in races as well, but somebody had to be among the last to finish....

Debrecen was a prosperous agricultural city, following the Calvinist creed.[8] Aside from a few major streets, people lived in small houses surrounded by large fences. In the wintertime, in the yards of each house haystacks would burn off the bristle of the slaughtered hogs.

In the summertime, on weekday afternoons, the maid took us to the Déri Park or to the Garden Park. The main attraction of the Déri Park was the many steps leading to the museum, inviting us to climb up and jump. The braver you were, the higher you climbed and the farther you jumped, well, the harder you fell! The Déri Park played an important role in my later life as well.[9]

The Garden Park, unlike the Déri Park, was a shady place full of old trees. I think we frequented this park because the friends of our maid went there too. This was not as much of a playground as the Déri Park. It had narrow roads and if I remember well, there was a statue in the middle.[10] When I picture this park, I see a snapshot of a disabled veteran who came there every day in his hand-driven elongated wheelchair. In the early 1930s one could see many disabled veterans in wheelchairs or, if they couldn't afford them, a piece of wood-panel to which four small wheels had been nailed to the bottom and which could be moved by hand as a mode of transportation.

---

8 About two-thirds of the inhabitants were Calvinists, one-fifth Catholics, and some 7.5 per cent were Jewish.

9 Established by Artúr Löfkovics, a local Jewish goldsmith and art collector in 1902, and significantly enhanced by the Jewish industrialist and philanthropist Frigyes Déri and his brother, György, the museum got a new building with a park and was named after the Déri family in 1928–1930.

10 Called Kálvin Square today, the Garden Park was a small park situated between the two emblematic Calvinist institutions: the Great Church and the College.

The forgotten victims of war. In a poor country, after a lost war, it is not good to be a disabled veteran.

~

Our family roots can be traced back to Spain and Turkey, prior to our lives in Hungary. My father was proud of his family; he came from a rabbinical family and sometimes talked about his ancestors. My grandfather's grandfather was a famous rabbi, and if you can believe family lore, in the distant past there was even a "miracle rabbi" in the family.[11] My paternal grandfather, József, was a bearded, devout Jew and my grandmother, Aranka (née Grünbaum), wore a wig as per the Orthodox Jewish tradition. My grandfather was a slim man with an upright posture, and my grandmother was a plump little woman. My father claimed that when my grandmother, who came from a wealthy family and was most likely of Ashkenazi origin, married my grandfather, she received a five-thousand-acre piece of land as a wedding present from her parents. That's the land my grandfather farmed, and he also owned a lumberyard in Hajdúdorog.[12] They brought up nine children — four boys and five girls — all of whom lived in the Debrecen area after they left home. Of my father's eight siblings, I recall only five — Erzsi, Irén, Rózsi, Róza and Ferenc — as we did not spend as much time with them as we did with my maternal family.

My mother's ancestors, the Deutsches, can be traced to the middle of the eighteenth century. They lived near Tokaj, a famous wine-producing area in Hungary. My maternal grandparents used to be well-to-do people. My maternal grandfather, whom I never knew because he died in 1920, owned a vineyard near Tokaj and a barrel factory and

---

1 The extended family included the Rabbi of Hajdúdorog, Samuel Frankel (1815–1881), an internationally renowned Torah scholar.
2 The house still exists there, and it is known as the Frenkel House.

a tavern in Sátoraljaújhely. My mother's features resembled those of my grandfather, whose picture I save in my desk drawer. He was a very good-looking man, and my mother inherited his nose, a "Deutsch-nose" as she called it (and sometimes she called it potato-nose).

My mother grew up in a large house in Sátoraljaújhely with her six siblings — Mihály, Jenő, Nándor, Etus, Szerén and Malvin. After my grandfather's death, my uncle Mihály took over the management of the vineyard. When Uncle Mihály got married, a new wing was added to my grandmother's house and that's where he lived with his wife, Manya, and their daughter, Anikó.

Before and during the war, I got to know my mother's family quite well over the summer and winter holidays. These visits took the form of what I called child exchanges: my cousin Imre from Törökszent-miklós would come to us for a couple of weeks every summer, and in return I would spend my Christmas holidays in Törökszentmiklós in the home of Aunt Etus and Uncle Sándor Rubinstein with my cousins Imre and Gyuri.[13]

My mother's sister and her family owned a printing shop and a stationery store on the main street, under the arcades. In the printing shop I could spend hours watching how the men set type and how the presses worked, and sometimes I would stand beside the calling card press as it opened and closed and I would have to feed the cards into the press at lightning speed. The bookstore was also one of my favourite spots. I would climb up the movable ladder to select a book from the shelf, and then I would perch on top of the ladder to read it. The store was a treasure trove of all kinds of books and papers, pens

---

13 Törökszentmiklós is a small agricultural town along the Debrecen-Budapest railway line. In the war years it had an Orthodox Jewish community of about five hundred. Sándor Rubinstein (1878–1945) was a paper merchant and typographer, as well as a trustee of the Orthodox Holy Society (Chevra Kadisha), a communal group that took responsibility for burying the dead. His printing press, one of the oldest and largest businesses in the region, also produced the local newspaper.

and pencils that I could pick up, look at and smell before putting them back.

Uncle Sándor was a devout man. Early in the morning, in the middle of winter, it was still dark when I had to go with him to the nearby little synagogue to pray. Getting up was incredibly difficult, but the little synagogue was warm and friendly. The *tefillin* was wound around the arm and the forehead and we all swayed to and fro in prayer. Back in Debrecen, praying was never as intimate and heartfelt as it was here. I remember the Havdalah ceremonies on Saturday evenings when my uncle led the service with a special braided candle. These religious rituals were very natural and not a burden. Before the meal, we would all wash hands and *bentch*, or bless, the meal. In the afternoons we used to read the paper, play Monopoly or study English from a record. The vacation was always over sooner than I would have liked.

We went to Ujhel (as we called Sátoraljaújhely) every summer from when I was six until I reached the age of eleven, and with the exception of one incident, I only have pleasant memories of the time spent there. Snippets of various experiences flash before my eyes: I see Grandma in front of the mirror in the morning as she is combing her long snow-white hair, which she wore in a bun on top; I'm playing in front of the flower garden when an ant bites me.

Ujhel is a border town. My grandmother's house was about fifty metres away from the Czechoslovak border. Between the two countries ran the Ronyva River, which was more like a small stream, and we could easily wade across it. Our excuse was to go there to go fishing, but really it was about the excitement of crossing into a foreign country. We didn't dare go further than a few metres toward Prague, but still, we were in Czechoslovakia, in unknown territory!

I liked to walk around the town on my own and when I was somewhat older, I used to run from my grandmother's house to the main street and back every morning. At the halfway point, I had to run across a bridge. Before the bridge, a crucified Christ looked down on me each time. Above his head was a plaque with the inscription INRI. Even at that age I knew that it meant he was the King of the Jews. I always arrived home panting and with a side stitch, needing to lie down to catch my breath. I considered this activity not so much a sport as an exercise in will power. Later on in life, I always put more emphasis on endurance than on speed.

My grandmother had a large house. There were even some unused rooms, which were locked up. From time to time I managed to peek inside and glimpse, in the semi-darkness, a lot of dusty sheet-covered furniture. Their topsy-turvy arrangement concealed bygone times. My clearest memory is of the dining room, with its large table and fringed tablecloth, a wardrobe against the wall, and an armchair near the window where my grandmother used to sit after the midday meal and watch the people passing by on the street. Now and then I too sat down onto its soft seat to observe the passersby through the open window.

The house had a backyard, or rather a garden. A path that ran through the middle of the garden was lined with mulberry trees. Sometimes I climbed them and I'd come away with black stains on my hands and face. At the front of the garden there was a stone table with stone benches around it, and about midway along the path a mangle — a machine that was used to wring laundry back in the day — was set up in an arbour that was more like a hiding place than a place of work. I never saw anyone using the mangle. The path carefully detoured around the mangle and continued on all the way to the back fence.

I spent a large part of the summer in the backyard. When I looked up at the sky, most of the time I would see a huge eagle circling slowly overhead. I was a bit scared because I'd heard once that an eagle was capable of snatching a child. From the yard you could also see a big mountain, on top of which stood a building. On some Sundays, the whole family would walk up the mountain.

On one particular Sunday visit — I think I was ten years old when this happened — my father was in Ujhel and he was sitting with my mother, my uncle's family and my grandma in an outdoor restaurant drinking beer when I decided to scout out the environs. I started out on a forest trail, which I later left and began running from one tree to the next. As I ran faster and faster down the steep slope, instead of being stopped by a tree, I was somehow propelled by it, and at first I was hurtling downward, then rolling at an ever increasing speed. Rolling, running, rolling… until finally, I have no idea how, I managed to stop. I was battered black and blue. For a while I could hardly breathe, but eventually I recovered. Let me add, that when I got up and looked around, I was shocked to find a precipice only a few metres in front of me. It wouldn't have taken much for me to go over the edge.

Limping but putting on a brave face, I returned to the restaurant where my father and the rest of the company were drinking their beer. By the time we got home, my leg was covered in bruises and swollen to twice its size. The doctor came over the next day and advised me to keep my leg elevated; he said the contusions would dissipate and all would be fine. I spent the next two weeks in a lounge chair in the garden with my leg resting up on cushions, but it didn't heal. I needed an operation on my leg to remove the pooled blood.

The doctors used chloroform to put me to sleep, which was an unforgettable experience. They put gauze and cotton balls soaked in chloroform over my face and made me breathe through them. Breathing became more and more difficult. I felt I was about to suffocate. I dreamt that I was run over by a tram. My mother gathered me up and took me home. Then I woke up.

There was a deep incision in my left leg right above the calf. At the outset, the doctor would pack a lot of gauze into it to soak up the accumulated fluid. The doctor changed the dressing every two or three days, and he removed the gauze from the wound amid loud wailing (I was doing the wailing). By the time the wound healed, I had forgotten how to walk on my left foot. For a while I used a crutch, then I switched to a cane. I spent the better part of the summer getting back on my feet, but by the time we returned to Debrecen I was pretty good at hobbling around. Since then I have learned that I suffer from a blood-factor deficiency that causes my blood to coagulate differently from normal. I have also learned that you shouldn't run from tree to tree on the mountainside, because you could roll off the mountain if the trees do not cooperate.

~

My parents were religious but not Orthodox; we kept a kosher household and since there was no kosher restaurant in Debrecen, we never ate in a restaurant. My parents wanted me to be able to read Hebrew when I reached the ripe old age of six. In the summertime, just before I started my first year of elementary school, my mother brought out a small table and two chairs to the front yard, and there I was introduced to the magical secret of the Hebrew letters. My teacher, a *bochur* with long, dangling curly sidelocks, couldn't have been more than twelve years old. Listening to my teacher was rather entertaining because, according to my mother, what she could hear all the time was, "Lafika, na! Lafika, na!" (Leslie, no!) However, it seems that the constant encouragement helped. When I got to school, I could read Hebrew very well.

Nowadays I do not pray frequently, but I will never forget how to read Hebrew. If I see the letters in a prayer book, the old elegant calligraphic shapes come back to me as I see those undulating beautiful letters.

My bar mitzvah was not a great affair. In the synagogue I was called to the Torah, where I sang the Maftir and made a *shnoder*, a donation pledge, for the benefit of the charity society of the school. Under the spread of the *tallis* the rabbi blessed me (along with the other bar mitzvah boys) and the service soon ended. My parents prepared a lunch for the teachers and for my friends and instantly I became an adult, with all the associated responsibilities.

After my bar mitzvah I prayed every morning at home for a long time in *tallis* and *tefillin*, though I later asked many questions that made my religiousness questionable. I felt I was a good Jew — I had a good voice and I even sang in the synagogue choir — but my God was not the one to whom we pray in the synagogue. I wrote a poem expounding my opinion, which unfortunately found its way to the teachers' office. Fortunately, they didn't expel me from the school; they didn't even punish me. I learned about this whole thing when my Hebrew teacher, talking about something else, cited a line from the poem. Otherwise, I was an active Jew, a Zionist, and when I was seventeen years old, I wanted to go to Eretz Yisrael, the Land of Israel, to be a kibbutznik, to build the country. I learned to speak Hebrew a little and I applied for a visa, but it was rejected.[14]

---

4 Although the founding father of Zionism, Theodor Herzl, was born in Budapest, the idea of Zionism had found few followers among Hungarian Jews before World War I. With the start of a new era characterized by antisemitism and anti-liberal state policies, more and more Hungarian Jews, especially the younger generations, were influenced by Zionist ideology. The movement of aliyah (immigration to Palestine, the "Holy Land") gained impetus in the second half of the 1930s due to a gradually darkening anti-Jewish atmosphere. However, immigration was severely restricted by British authorities; only a few thousand permits were distributed in Hungary and applicants had to meet various criteria, such as participation in preparatory camps. Furthermore, with the outbreak of war, leaving the country became increasingly difficult.

A False Calm

When I was fourteen or fifteen, I got to go to both Kassa (now Košice, Slovakia) as an "exchange child," and to Budapest for the first time in my life.

During a Boy Scout meeting in Debrecen, a senior scout showed up for an inspection and asked us all kinds of questions. I must have given the right answer to one of his questions because afterward he went over to our troop leader (who told me about this later on) and suggested that I be sent to a camp for leaders. The next camp was going to be held on Hárs Hill in Budapest for one week in the middle of winter, and I was one of several chosen to attend. It was so cold that we almost froze to death, but it was a great experience nonetheless.

Since I was already in Budapest, I was invited over to my aunt Szerén's home. My aunt was married to Dezső Teitelbaum and they had two children, Márta and Leslie. My cousin Márta was engaged to a very wealthy cloth merchant by the name of Bohrer, and once, when I went for a walk on the boulevard with them, they bought me potato chips at the Western Railway Station.[1] (It's fascinating how such

---

Most probably, they had the chips at the Ilkovics Buffet, the first fast-food restaurant in Budapest, established by the Jewish businessman Izidor Ilkovics in 1925 on the Grand Boulevard (Nagykörút) right across from the railway station.

trivialities are lodged in one's memory, while more important things completely escape us.) Budapest seemed wonderful to me, with its gigantic apartment buildings and its heavy traffic.

Of course, we invited Márta to our home the following summer. She was an extraordinarily beautiful girl, and men — regardless of race or religion — were all crazy about her. On more than one occasion, they would serenade her at night under our window. The fact that ours was the only house on the street where the Roma (then called Gypsy) played[2] made me extremely proud.

In June 1941, there was a bomb attack in Kassa, where some of my relatives lived.[3] By then, Kassa belonged to Hungary again; Czechoslovakia was all divided up.[4] The region still enjoyed its democratic nature, and you could still observe this in the city and its people. I landed in a free and happy environment that possessed a vibrant and cultivated social life.[5] Right after the bombing, my cousin Klári, who was an only child, came to see us in Debrecen. I think her parents, my uncle Nándor and aunt Fridka, assumed that Kassa was a likely target for bombing — and this proved to be true — while Debrecen was not. At least, no one had started bombing Debrecen yet. We went to the outdoor pool frequently and we had lots of fun.

---

2 Many of the Roma in Hungary made a living by performing music, and therefore, in this context, "Gypsy" was used as a synonym for musician.

3 On June 26, 1941, unidentified warplanes, supposedly a Soviet unit, bombed Kassa, which offered a pretext for Hungary to join Hitler's invasion of the Soviet Union on the following day.

4 In 1938–1939, Czechoslovakia fell victim to Nazi expansion, and its territory was divided among its neighbours. As a result, Hungary regained some of its former territories, including the southern strip of the territory that is Slovakia today, including the city of Kassa/Košice.

5 The interwar Czechoslovak Republic was indeed a democratic state if compared to other (more authoritarian, even dictatorial) regimes in interwar Central and Eastern Europe. Despite the culturally diverse and open character of society, Czechoslovak democracy had certain shortcomings, especially in the field of minority rights.

When Klári returned to Kassa, I accompanied her. Although Klári was a year older and going out with older boys, she proved to be a good friend to me. We would plan activities for every day. One Sunday, the whole family went to a restaurant. I think this was the first time that I ever had a meal in a restaurant. My uncle carefully wiped his cutlery clean and before ordering, he asked me what I'd like to eat. My uncle Nándor was a bank manager, and he and his family lived in a small but attractive house, which they owned. When Klári and I stayed at home, we would read a book by Vaszary together and have a great laugh.[6]

~

As I mentioned, my brother, Gyuri, was four years younger than me, and I believe I made him aware of my seniority. I don't think there was ever any competition between the two of us. As the younger, he felt he had to defer to his older brother. This was reinforced by the fact that I was a good student while he was not. When I became a leader in the Boy Scouts, he was a member in my group. I think he was actually rather proud of me and did not feel at all envious. The downside was that he wasn't even trying to do better and catch up with me. I think this was largely my fault. I tutored my classmates but didn't make time for him. My math teacher kept warning me that if Gyuri got a bad mark, he would enter it on my record. At the time I thought this was ridiculous, but now I'm convinced that it would have been the right approach. Perhaps that way I would have come to my senses and become a better brother. Our "separate" lives were a result of having separate friends, separate activities and separate interests due to the four-year age difference. When we were young, we used to play together a lot, but later on, we only saw one another at home at mealtimes and in the evenings.

---

6 Gábor Vaszary (1897–1985), a Hungarian writer and journalist. His humorous and witty novels were internationally known and very popular in the 1930s and 1940s. His bestseller, *Monpti*, was translated into twenty-eight languages.

I attended a Jewish high school and it was compulsory to participate in the Friday evening and Saturday morning services. The Saturday mornings would start off with a service in the small temple on Kápolnási Street;[7] the students led the prayers and the whole congregation sang together. The melodies were beautiful and some of them resound in my ears to this day. The high school boys sat on the ground floor and the girls sat in the balcony behind lace curtains. The girls were able to peek through the curtains, but when we looked up, we couldn't see anything but the curtains. The service ended before noon, and afterward our group always went to the Déri garden to walk the paths.

Later, a fine Saturday meal would be waiting for us at home: cholent with the traditional kugel on the bottom. When the kugel was first revealed, it boasted a gorgeous brown colour, the grease gleaming on its surface. The next thing to be removed from the bean dish was the hard-boiled egg with its brown-tinted shell, which is soon turned into *Eier mit Zwiebel*, eggs with onions. Beck the baker would make the cholent, putting it in the oven on Friday so it would be ready for our housemaid to pick up on Saturday at noon.

I don't have many memories left from my high school years, in spite of the fact that this was one of the most important periods of my life. That's when my character was formed and that's when I decided to become an engineer and to later settle down and start a family. That's when I came to love studying and realized that through knowledge and strength of will I could achieve anything I wanted in life. I learned this from my father, who always told me that when a Jew has to flee, the only thing he can take with him is the knowledge in his head; that is his true wealth and the only way he can obtain it is through studying.

---

7 The Kápolnási Street Synagogue, with its six hundred seats, was called "small" because the Status Quo congregation had a larger synagogue on the main street of Debrecen (1896–1965). The second temple was built in 1909 and still serves the local community.

The subjects that interested me most were mathematics, physics and natural sciences. I was a great admirer of Freudian psychology and I later became quite knowledgeable about the topic. I was so interested in the interpretation of dreams that I began by analyzing my own dreams, then went on to analyze those of my friends with great enthusiasm. In addition, I was fond of literature and derived a lot of enjoyment from it. I tried my hand at writing poetry. My friend Gyuri Kemény, who chose at a young age to become a writer, tried his best to lure me over to this field but in the end, I stuck to my original decision and went into sciences. We were best friends in high school, and I knew that his father was an alcoholic. He and his mother lived with his grandmother, who supported herself (and them) by dividing up her two-room apartment into small cubicles partitioned by blankets, which she rented out to night lodgers. Gyuri and I used to play bridge in one of these cubicles, I guess the one that he and his mother shared.

Gyuri used to carry a small notebook in which he would jot down anything odd or unusual that occurred at school. This notebook was a treasure trove of students' witticisms, teachers' bloopers and minor pranks. When we had a free period, we would always ask Gyuri to read some of the entries from his notebook. He'd laugh the hardest at the jokes and as he did, his Adam's apple would bob up and down.

In addition to Gyuri, quite a few others — Gabi Horovitz, Laci Kepes, Gyuri Gergely — belonged to my close circle of friends. Then there was Peti Kálmánczi, whose father was a farm manager out in the countryside while he, his mother and his sister lived in Debrecen, because that's where the high school was located. The Kálmánczis were also poor, not that it had any effect on our friendship. They lived in an apartment house, and their two rooms were on opposite sides of a long corridor; their kitchen was not connected to either of those rooms, and the "small room" was the afternoon meeting place for our group. The main reason for this was that Zsuzsi, Peti's younger sister, was an invalid. She'd had polio when she was a young child and as a consequence walked with great difficulty and had a limp. Tomi

Szemere was courting her and had they not both perished during the war, perhaps they would have gotten married.[8]

Thanks to Zsuzsi, some girls were also part of our little group, like her best friend Ági Losonczi, and in the afternoons the small room was always filled with boys and girls. Also, through my cousin Klári Kovács, who was two years younger than me, I was acquainted with another group of girls. With those girls we would stroll in countless circuits around the garden of the Déri Museum, the other meeting place of our group. Interactions between the boys and the girls were very congenial. The notion of sexual relationships never even crossed our minds in those days. The rumour that a girl had been seen kissing was the sort of thing you would only speak about in whispers.

The garden of the Déri Museum was where we went when the weather was good, generally with a book tucked under our arms so we'd have something to do in case we were the only ones to show up. It would take a while for the whole group to assemble. Nothing was arranged in advance, but we knew exactly whom we would find there. The boys would arrive, and then the girls. Small groups would form and we'd start "making circuits." There were long conversations. Every teacher was picked apart and every book that we were all reading simultaneously was discussed.

The library was also in the Déri Museum. The small blue requisition form on which we wrote down the books we wanted to read cost only a few fillérs. A side entrance led to the library's waiting room, which could seat ten to fifteen people. All of a sudden, a window

---

8   Unlike the author's family, the Kálmánczis were deported to Auschwitz. At the Birkenau selection ramp, seventeen-year-old Zsuzsi, as a disabled person, and her mother, Irén, as a woman in her early fifties, were most likely sent to the gas chamber immediately. Lajos Kálmánczi and his son, Péter (Peti), were transferred to other camps to work for the war effort, and both of them perished in 1945, Lajos in Bergen-Belsen and Péter in Buchenwald. Tamás (Tomi) Szemere was also deported to Auschwitz and murdered.

would open and the forms would be collected. After a further wait, the window would open again and our names read out. Everyone received one of the books on the form and the title was crossed out. I still remember the winter evenings when it was nice and warm in the waiting room and the regulars could have a pleasant conversation while waiting for their books.

The library also had a reading room. Here too the books were not accessible, and you had to ask for them. You also had to tiptoe around and were not allowed to talk. Sometimes, when I got a humorous book, I wanted to laugh, but I was only allowed to smile. I recall reading *Mein Kampf* and a few books on graphology there (neither of which fell into the category of "humorous"). However, on reading *Mein Kampf*, I didn't think its ultimate consequence would be to question my right to live. First, because I was accustomed to antisemitic rants; second, it was not antisemitism originating from Hungary; and third, I considered it a political manifesto rather than a government program. Besides, no one tends to believe very bad news about themself.

I don't remember reading any other specific titles. On cold Saturday mornings in winter and on rainy summer afternoons, we took refuge there in the reading room if we had nothing else to do.

For a number of years, starting when I was about twelve, I attended dance classes on Saturday afternoons. Everyone would be all dressed up and the girls smelled good. We learned how to dance the tango and the foxtrot and, for the final exam, the quadrille, a type of square dance. When we were older, we had afternoon parties. The girls hosted these parties and there were tables laden with fine pastries. The music was played on a gramophone and we danced to the latest hits. These parties continued even when the war was raging and when our younger teachers were drafted and swallowed up one after the other by the forced labour camps in the Ukraine. They came back from time to time to teach, and then they returned to the horrors, which they never talked to us about. Then one of our teachers,

Zoltán Weiszman, a very talented young teacher of natural sciences and chemistry, did not return. He disappeared in the Ukraine; the war devoured him. The majority of our teachers belonged to an older age group and therefore could stay home. Thus, in the Debrecen Jewish high school, classes continued until March 1944.

However, attending school was not without its problems. The second floor of our high school was occupied by the Hungarian army for their military offices,[9] and only a few classrooms and the adjoining temple were available for teaching purposes (supposedly, according to Jewish religious law, one must not convert a study hall into a temple but one is allowed to convert a temple into a study hall. Perhaps that's why the temple in Yiddish is called the *shul*, meaning school.) The desks were set up in the lobby of the temple and that's where we studied in two shifts: one in the morning, the other in the afternoon.

Although the real horrors of the war didn't touch us until March 1944, we heard and knew many details. We listened to the English radio broadcasts every day and followed the troop movements on the map that hung on the wall of our room — first, into the Soviet Union and later out of the Soviet Union when the Germans started to retreat in order to "shorten the front."[10] We heard about the Warsaw Ghetto Uprising in 1943, and we knew that the men who had been sent to the Ukraine for labour service would often not make it home alive. We also heard about the total defeat of the Hungarian army at Voronezh, and that those who survived it were fleeing back to Hungary whichever way they could.[11] We heard about Stalingrad and knew for

---

9   In wartime, the army assumed special powers to requisition schools and other community buildings in order to quarter troops.

10 "Shorten the front" was one of the euphemisms used by Axis propaganda to deceive the public about inevitable military defeat.

11 At Voronezh, in January 1943, the Soviet Red Army broke through the front line of the Hungarian Second Army as part of the offensive to encircle German troops at Stalingrad. At least half of the two hundred thousand Hungarian soldiers either

certain that the Germans were going to lose the war. The one thing we didn't know was what fate awaited us and whether we Hungarian Jews would survive this world conflagration. Our teacher Dr. Gonda phrased the situation as follows: It's true that Hitler is about to kick the bucket, but first he'll kick us.[12]

In the meantime, we kept on going to school, and our major preoccupation was whether we were adequately prepared for the next day's math or literature quiz. Our school and our parents shielded us from the horrors. Both we and our parents were hopeful that what had occurred elsewhere in Europe would not happen in Hungary.

We courted girls and enjoyed an active social life. I started dating Judit, my wife-to-be. We would go to the movies and the theatre, study together, read books, discuss politics and debate important topics. From time to time, we played bridge, and if we misplayed a hand, we got upset. We tried to remain as normal as possible in an upside-down, abnormal world. You can get used to anything... Even the war. And the Jew-hating. And the fact that it was dangerous to walk in certain areas in the evening.

It was well into the middle of the war when, on one snowy winter evening, I took my camera outside — I'd had it since age fourteen, and photography was one of my hobbies. I set up the equipment under a streetlamp and opened the diaphragm to take a long exposure picture of a well, on top of which a thick layer of sparkling snow glistened in the ghostly lamplight. Suddenly a police officer showed up and asked me what I was doing. I told him that I was taking a picture of the well. He couldn't fathom why anyone would want to photograph a well on a winter evening. He said that if I didn't stop right away, he

---

died, were wounded or went missing over the course of a few days, including thousands of Jewish labour servicemen.

12 László Gonda (1910–1985) was a historian and a teacher of history, Latin and French at the Jewish Gymnasium in Debrecen between 1934 and 1944. After the war, he immigrated to Israel.

would take me to the police station. I packed up the equipment and went home. So yes, it was dangerous to move around in certain areas.

My main job at the time was studying. My father's wisdom was always on my mind. He had always been proud of having matriculated from the Debrecen School of Commerce. In 1943, my class matriculated, and I applied to the Faculty of Science at the University of Debrecen, where I was admitted because I had finished high school with an A average.[13] Jews were no longer being admitted as regular university students, but four of us enrolled as guest students, studying together and doing well on our exams.[14]

I was interested in everything that science had to offer. My passion was modern physics — atomic theory, Bohr with his electrons in constant motion, nuclear fission, relativity and so on. I always liked mathematics and I wanted to become a mechanical engineer from quite a young age. Secretly I was hoping that I would be the one to invent *perpetuum mobile*, perpetual motion. I also dabbled in graphology and anytime I saw some handwriting, I started analyzing it right away.

Once the German occupation began, we were not allowed to enter the main building of the university. However, some of our professors relocated the lectures to a secondary building for our sake, which took quite a bit of courage on their part.

～

13 Out of 23 students in László's class, one matriculated with special merits (A+), two with A, including László, the others got a B+ or a lower grade. *Yearbook of the Debrecen Jewish Gymnasium*, 1942–1943.

14 This status was one of the ways to circumvent the regulations of the so-called Numerus Clausus Law. The number of Jews admitted as regular students was limited to a mere 6 per cent, but some of those excluded from this cohort could still attend courses as visiting (or guest) students.

At some point in the 1940s, my father was called up for labour service. He arrived at an assembly point near Debrecen with the requisite amount of gear.[15] We didn't hear from him for weeks, and then we received a message that we could visit him if we wished. My mother took me along. We boarded a train early in the morning and arrived before noon in the village where my father was being detained.

It was a very strange visit. My father was made to stand on an elevation behind a barbed-wire fence, while we stood on the other side of the fence, watching him stand motionless and mute on top of the little hill, looking at us. It was forbidden to talk or wave. We could only watch him, and we felt that he was bound for death. I don't remember what went through my mind at the time. This "meeting" must have been horrible for my parents.[16]

Unexpectedly, my father was allowed to return home a few days later. Perhaps it was because of his age, since he was already in his forty-eighth year. That's how he survived: as a result of the strange and incomprehensible games that fate plays.

In Debrecen, my age group was not called up for labour service at this time, but on May 1, 1944, I wound up in a labour camp. Earlier on in the forced labour service call-ups, decorated Jewish veterans of World War I had been accorded special status, and the father of my good friend Tomi Szemere was a lieutenant who had been exempted from service. Now, he somehow managed to arrange for his son, along with a few of his son's friends, to be in Haláp[17] under his

---

5 The conscription centre was in Püspökladány, a small town on the Budapest-Debrecen railway line.

6 Before Hungary entered the war in 1941, treatment of Jews in labour service was relatively lenient, if compared to their wartime sufferings. It is not clear why Leslie's father was punished in such a strange way, but harsh disciplinary measures were not unusual in the armies of the era.

7 A forest in the vicinity of Debrecen owned by the city.

command to work in the forest there. Compared to people in other labour camps, we lived like lords. We were billeted in farmhouses, where others cleaned and cooked for us. All we did from morning till night was "cricketing," which meant freeing the roots of felled trees from the soil. We worked with shovels and pickaxes,[18] and after four weeks, all beefed up, tanned and healthy, we had to return to Debrecen.

---

18 In fact, the task described as an easy adventure was very hard physical labour.

Lives in Suspension

In June, we were sent to the Debrecen ghetto. In the ghetto, each family was allocated one room, which they filled with all the belongings they wanted to salvage, so there was hardly any space left for the people. Since it was June, everyone was out on the streets most of the time. The few city blocks into which Debrecen's Jewish population had been crammed were now teeming with throngs of people.

After a few weeks, the ghetto was evacuated, and everyone was herded to a brick factory carrying only small knapsacks. It was late afternoon when we started off. We were moving westward, and the reddish sun slanted its rays at us. It was close to dark when we arrived at our new quarters. The gendarmes herded us up to the attic of a barn. By then it was completely dark and everyone tried to secure just enough room to lie down. There was quarrelling and fighting all around, and it was a long time before the four of us could spread a blanket on the dusty floor and finally lie down.

The first thing I did the next morning was leave the attic and look for some place to stay outdoors. Judit's family squeezed even closer together, and when it looked like four more people could fit in with them, I went back to the attic for my family and we all moved over. Fortunately, it wasn't raining, because our spot was underneath the eaves, and the eaves covered only half of our "apartment," which consisted of a blanket with four bedcovers and four pillowcases.

Both in the ghetto and in the brick factory, we were surrounded by friends and acquaintances. And Judit was always there. We couldn't even imagine what might lie in store for us and didn't even dare think about the future. We lived only for the present; everything else was relegated to the background.

We didn't spend many days in that place, but every day was filled with atrocities. The wealthier citizens of Debrecen were taken to the gendarmerie station and tortured until they disclosed where they had hidden their gold and jewellery, if they possessed any. I had to give up the one birthday present that my uncle from Ujhel had sent me for my bar mitzvah, a nice wristwatch that my mother told me had cost forty pengő.[1] The Hungarian official told me that I would not need it anyway.

Gradually, the prospect of leaving this place behind began to seem like redemption to us, no matter the destination. The first transport had already left and we wanted to get on the next transport at all costs. We succeeded in that.

I learned later that the first transport set out in the direction of Auschwitz but for some reason turned back and then started off toward Vienna. It took the train four or five days to arrive at Strasshof, just outside Vienna. Those of us in the next transport headed west right away and reached Strasshof after a two-day journey. In the railcar there was just enough room to sit, so we tried to sleep while sitting. The night was filled with wailing, crying, moaning and bickering. For the purpose of relieving ourselves, a bucket was supplied, which you couldn't really make use of in the dark of the night. Another transport, which consisted of doctors, lawyers and others who had been staying in the attic, was taken to Auschwitz — I later

---

1 According to the exchange rate at the time, the watch costed approximately one hundred and fifty Canadian dollars.

learned that first deporting the "upper crust," the leaders of a Jewish community, to the death camps was a common tactic of the Nazis. Two other transports left from the Debrecen transit camp, all headed to Auschwitz.

It was late in the afternoon of the second day when our train arrived at its final destination of Strasshof. German soldiers surrounded the train and made us exit the cars quickly. My family and Judit's had travelled in the same car, and the first thing I did on arrival was set out with Judit in search of water, a pail in hand. We found water nearby, filled up the vessel, and returned to our families. By the time we reached them, there was no water left in the vessel. We were so thirsty we drank it all on the way back.

Strasshof was a distribution centre, and the Jews who arrived there were to be directed to various workplaces. In the first days after the deportation, my grandfather died of starvation in Strasshof; he would not eat anything because the food was not kosher. My grandmother had died of a heart attack on March 8, eleven days before Germany occupied Hungary. At least she did not have to suffer the humiliations that my grandfather was made to endure.

After this tragedy, me and my family were sent to a tank factory; Judit and her family were sent to do farm work. In the Lager of the Saurer Werke factory we lived amid different nationalities and worked at night.[2]

The factory was located on the east side of the city, not more than thirty kilometres from the Hungarian border. It contained a large Lager where the *Ostarbeiter*, the Eastern European forced labourers, stayed. The Lager itself was organized under the authority of the SS, but the people and their maintenance were the responsibility of the

2 Besides Jewish deportees, millions of POWs and civil forced labourers from all over Hitler's Europe performed slave labour in the German war industry.

factory. For lodging, there were well-kept wooden barracks. The La-ger was well-guarded but not fenced off; the SS had an office at the gate of the Lager, and the people could, for a good reason, exit and re-enter.

In the middle of the Lager was the barrack where the Jews lived, about one hundred and fourteen of us. A wooden fence separated this barrack, but it served only a symbolic role and was not exactly an obstacle, not like keeping prisoners within a prison. The authorities knew that the Jews had nowhere else to go anyway. The gate of our fence was locked with a key and unlocked by someone from Saurer Werke, who took us to work and brought us back. But in case of an air raid, I think another key was kept by the man who was head of our Lager.

We had to work from eight-thirty at night to seven-thirty in the morning. The food was the same as that received by the Ger-man workers — meat three times a week — and the barrack was well heated and supplied with a flush toilet, an area to wash laundry and a place to clean ourselves.

The daily air raids were the biggest dangers to our lives, and we were absolutely sure that sooner or later, a bomb would finish off our lives. The bombs fell at daytime, often mornings, and so after about two hours of sleep, we had to get up and go to the air-raid shelter. The other fear — and we didn't even dare to think about it often — was that when the end of the war neared, how would the whole thing end for us? If by chance we survived the bombing, would we survive the German collapse and the Soviet victory as well?

When my brother and I were young, we spent our time fighting rather than playing, and often we were not really a part of each other's lives. But during the deportation, when I was nineteen, he was almost sixteen, and we grew closer. We both worked the night shift in the tank factory, but it was mostly the worrying about our parents that bonded us. Our mother, who once had such beautiful, thick, black and wavy hair, was becoming rather frail. Every day she was assigned to peeling potatoes, and it was the potatoes she stole that made feeding our family — aside from her — easier. My mother claimed she was never hungry, so we would eat her portion as well. Our father had been suffering from a stomach ailment for a long time. It was mostly our mother who tended to him, and we were worried about him as well.

From our time in the Lager, we learned that the German soldier is the horribly perfect creation of Hitler. If ordered to kill, he would kill; he would kill a child or a defenseless woman without any particular emotion or feeling of guilt. If he didn't receive an order, he wouldn't kill.

Something we experienced may serve as a case in point. During our stay, we were not under the jurisdiction of the SS. Right beside our Lager, however, there was another Lager behind barbed wire where Jews just like us, as well as others, were kept under the authority of the SS. In the last month of the war, every evening five of us from our Lager went to work in the same factory as the "stripers," the men wearing striped prisoner uniforms. The only difference was that the stripers were escorted by SS men, who would surround them with weapons at the ready and put them under floodlights to prevent their escape. Three SS officers marched behind the group, and behind the SS officers came the five of us. We had no guard and no supervision. We only used the light of those floodlights to help us avoid falling into bomb craters. Sometimes the SS officers would turn to us and begin to engage us in conversation. The yellow star was there on our chests, so it wasn't as if they didn't know that the only reason we were working in the factory was that we were Jews. If anyone among the stripers stepped out of formation, the same officer who was discussing the story of that day's air attack with us would have shot the escapee without hesitation, simply because he had been ordered to do so. They didn't have any instructions concerning us, so we could do as we pleased. We weren't their responsibility, and even though we were Jewish, that wasn't their problem, only ours.

In the Saurer Werke, I documented this important period of my life in a diary, and I wrote to Judit when I could. I had given Judit's name, and the names of her family members, to a woman from the Red Cross who visited our Lager. I told her they were probably in Vienna because we had been in the same transport, and I asked her to inquire about them wherever she went. This woman — blessed be her name — promised she would, and she did find them, and gave Judit our address. The next time the Red Cross woman came to our barrack, I learned that Judit and her family were in Aspern.[3]

I knew that if somebody from our Lager was sick, he or she would be going to the same hospital as the people from Aspern, and I knew a man named Mr. Auspitz in the hospital. The next time somebody from our Lager was sent there, I told him to give my letter to Mr. Auspitz and to ask him to forward it to anyone who was in the hospital from Aspern. Soon after that, Judy and I were able to be in touch. This correspondence kept us together almost to the last days in our most difficult time.

By reading the diary and the letters that Judy and I exchanged with each other, one would think that our deportation wasn't so terrible after all. The fact is that in June 1944, approximately 15,000 Hungarian Jews were deported to Vienna and its vicinity. For some reason, these people were treated differently from other Jews, and most of them survived. We were part of this large number of Jews, and we survived partly because of the special treatment we received and partly, I think, because in April 1945, we escaped from the Lager as the Soviet Red Army was approaching it.

---

3   The SS allowed the Red Cross to provide the prisoners with social aid, mostly medicine and clothes.

Our fates were unknown, as illustrated here by a quote from the last entry in my deportation diary, on April 2: *The front line is inching closer and closer. Now we can hear shots being fired here and there, and the horizon is tinged red at noon. Everyone is agitated, and there is tension in the air. … We do not even have air-raid alerts anymore.*

Earlier, our barrack was bombed and had collapsed. Our new barrack was not in the Lager proper anymore. It was on the other side of the road and was not fenced in. Otherwise, it was the same as the old one, just without everything we had before. But at least we were alive.

And then, on April 6, 1945, an unexpected, unbelievable visitor entered the barrack. "I am the Director of Saurer Werke," he said. He was alone, with a big trunk in his hand, like a suitcase. He came, he said, to take leave from the workers who had done a good job for the factory. With that, he opened the trunk, which was full of chocolates and cigarettes, and distributed them, giving something to everybody. And then he left, driving away in his car.

It is difficult to describe the effect of that event. Everybody had a different interpretation of this unannounced visit. Was the war over? Did he want to save his skin so that if the Soviets came, we would say that he was a good guy? Was he the director at all? How would this visit affect us? Would they treat us better? And so on, and so on.

There was no work that night, and the guards had already started to leave. I was lying in my bed trying to figure out what this visit was about. I liked history and I read a lot of books, and from Greek mythology an old story of the Trojan horse and Helen of Troy came to mind, along with its well-known saying: "Beware of Greeks bearing gifts." This referred to the wooden horse offered by the Greeks to their enemies, the Trojans; when the horse was pulled into the city of Troy, the Trojans believed it to be a gift of surrender, but it instead held armed soldiers hidden inside…and it resulted in the Trojans losing their ten-year war. And what if the story of gift-givers applied here too? If a German bearing gifts comes to you….

As I mentioned, we had been taken out of our bombed-out Lager, to the other side of the road where the factory was located. Outside the controlled Lager area, it would have been easy for them to do with us what they wished. But it was also easy to escape! No fence, no Lager SS. Would anyone use this opportunity to escape? A weighty thought: Is it possible? Shall I learn from history? Here I am, practically free, and if I want, I can use it. Should I follow this option and escape and liberate myself? Do something or continue to be a helpless prisoner, ready to follow the orders of my enemy?

I could not sleep that night. Early in the morning, my family — except for my father, who was in the hospital in Vienna and about to undergo a serious operation — walked out of the barrack with our relatives the Kovács and another family, closed the door and, taking measured steps, not too fast, not too slow, started to go toward our freedom. Most of the people we had been living with for nine months remained in the barrack. Much later, we learned that these people eventually perished, another one hundred unfortunate souls, victims of human evil. These friends of ours were counting the days until the end of the war, full of anxiety and happiness that the war would soon end and they would be able to go home. For them, it didn't happen that way.[4]

If our "Greek" hadn't shown up with chocolates and cigarettes as gifts in hand, if on this day nothing special had happened, I would not have evoked the story of Troy, and I too would have died.

---

4   Several of Leslie's fellow prisoners did fall victim to massacres committed right before the end of the war, including the one at Hofamt Priel (see the introduction about this). However, many others survived the war.

After the Storm

It is difficult to say what the exact date of our liberation was, since it didn't happen all at once. When we escaped, we ended up in the cellar of a liqueur factory with other deportees, mainly with people from the neighbouring Lager. They had arrived there via Auschwitz. They told us what they had been through, and only then did we realize what had happened to the Jews of Europe. Some of these people had lived through many concentration camps, had to survive in them for three or four years.

These former prisoners knew where we had come from and they took care of feeding us, as all we had managed to bring with us was a rucksack full of bread that we had saved in the previous days, nothing else. Water was in short supply so we drank wine. Wine and spirits were everywhere but nobody was drunk. We washed our hands in spirits. There was a sense of freedom already, but no one wanted to leave the cellar yet. Outside, there was still war. We knew that we were free but we really didn't feel it. We knew that eventually we would go home, but we didn't get going. Our father was not with us and we didn't know what to do. A front line separated us.

For now, a small nook of the factory's cellar was our abode, but at least we were safe. The Germans didn't dare to come into the cellar. They were afraid — and rightly so — of their former prisoners.

I next remember the day of April 9 — that day, a Russian soldier ripped off the yellow star from my shirt. I'd had to wear a yellow star since April 5, 1944 — one year and four days. This symbolical act gave me back my freedom and my life. This day was our Passover, our liberation from the bondage in Germany. (And on April 9, 1924, exactly twenty-one years earlier in Hungary, my mother and father had gotten married. Hallelujah!)

As soon as we could, we left for Hungary to get out of the war zone — the battle for Vienna raged on from April 2 to 13, 1945. We were afraid of the Germans returning and we were also fearful of the wild Soviet soldiers. I think we started our way home on April 11, not realizing, then, that it was our mother's birthday. She turned forty-nine years old. One time, a Russian soldier wanted to take my mother away, and my brother stayed by her side and protected her from being taken.[1]

On our journey home, the main danger continued to be the Russian soldiers. They tried, a few times, to capture me and my cousin Steve (Pista) to take us to forced labour. We always managed to escape. If we had not, we could have ended up in a Soviet labour camp in Ukraine, like some of our friends who came home three years later.

From Vienna, we had started off with a good cart and four horses that we had gotten from the Russians — by the time we arrived in Győr, all we had left was a blind horse and a wrecked cart, because whenever we met Russian soldiers en route, they always exchanged our horses for their poorer ones.

From Győr, we continued our odyssey by train, eventually arriving in Budapest, where we stayed at the home of our aunt Szerén. Her whole family had survived and they were so very happy to see us. While we were there, we learned about the death of President Roosevelt. Interestingly, his death was soon followed by the death of

---

1   Committing atrocities like looting, rape and other arbitrary acts was commonplace in the Red Army, despite harsh discipline, and this violence did not spare Jewish survivors, either.

Hitler; both men had started and finished their political lives as leaders in the same years, 1933–1945.

Finally, we arrived back in Debrecen. My old friend Gyuri Kemény was waiting at the train station. He had been going every day to meet the train from Budapest, to see who was arriving back from hell.

Our old house was still there but another family was living in it. We received one room to move into. We were home. In those first days, Mother cut the roses in the garden and we sold them to a flower shop to put bread on the table. Soon after, Imre got me a job at a newspaper where I used my meagre knowledge of shorthand to take war reports from the radio. The pay was enough to buy food.

Three weeks after we had arrived in Debrecen, my fifteen-year-old brother, Gyuri, left Hungary by asking some Soviet soldiers for a lift on their truck, went back to Vienna and brought back our father, who up until that point had been convinced that we were among the murdered. My father felt unimaginable joy and delight when he caught sight of his child entering the hospital ward. He believed that Gyuri saved his life. The truth is that our father saved ours. If he had been with us in the Lager and had not been strong enough to leave with us at the right moment, we would have shared the doom of our Lager mates.

After the war, from my father's immediate family that I recall, only my father and three of his sisters, Erzsi, Irén and Rózsi, along with their families, returned to Debrecen. My father's brother Ferenc Frenkel and my father's sister Róza Steinberger had been deported and did not survive.

From my mother's family in Törökszentmiklós, my older cousin Gyuri, who had been called up for labour service in 1943, never returned. His wife and son survived and went to Israel. Imre, my younger cousin and good friend, was also in the labour service, but he made it home. Tragically, he died of some sort of blood disease in 1945. I visited him shortly before his death. My aunt Etus knew that her son's disease was incurable, and she shared this information with me. It was an awful visit, since I knew that I was talking with someone who was condemned to death. Imre was cheerful and we had a pleasant conversation. Perhaps he didn't know what fate awaited him. We didn't talk about his illness. He died soon after this, and somewhat later, his father, Uncle Sándor, followed. He had stomach cancer. Aunt Etus, in whose company I spent so many happy times in Törökszentmiklós, was left on her own. Their old house had been hit by a bomb during the war and she lived the rest of her days mostly alone, as a co-tenant in an apartment shared with strangers. She outlived her family by more than thirty years, eventually dying of cancer. Whenever I travelled back to Hungary from Canada, I always visited her. She was my mother's only sibling in Hungary and it was a pleasure to chat with her.

My aunt Szerén and her family in Budapest were not deported and they survived the storm in the Budapest ghetto. Later they immigrated to Israel, except for my cousin Márta, who divorced her cloth-merchant husband and got married for a second time. Her second husband died in the mid-1980s, and she now lives by herself in Budapest. She owns a villa in Rózsadomb, where we have a standing invitation.[2] We stay in touch with her, and one summer, she visited us in Toronto.

My other three maternal uncles perished, as did one of my maternal aunts. My uncle Jenő Deutsch died as a partisan in the forests near Miskolc, Hungary; his wife, Klári, and daughter, Ági, were deported to Auschwitz, where Ági was murdered; my uncle Mihály Deutsch was randomly shot in a "decimation" (unluckily, and randomly, being tenth in a row)[3] in a forced labour camp, and neither

---

2 Rózsadomb ("Rose Hill") in District II of Budapest is a residential quarter with villas, inhabited by the upper middle class and the elite.

3 Decimation — the summary execution of every tenth member of the unit — was a brutal method of military discipline originating from Roman times. In the Hungarian army in World War II the method was formally illegal, but occasionally employed, mostly against labour servicemen.

his wife, Manya, nor their daughter, Anikó, survived the war; and my uncle Nándor and aunt Fridka shared the fate of so many other Hungarian Jews: they died in Auschwitz-Birkenau. Their daughter, my cousin Klári, fled before the deportation and for a while she was in hiding in Budapest. In the end, she perished, too. My aunt Malvin, who had lived in a part of Slovakia, was lost to us already before the German occupation of Hungary. She and her daughter, also named Klári, had been deported after Germany occupied Czechoslovakia, and were murdered in one of the Nazi camps.

After the war, some of my friends made it back to Debrecen from different Nazi camps. When Laci Kepes found out that I had become a Zionist he embraced me, but when I was in Israel many years later and looked him up at his office, he acted as if he'd never met me. When I told him that we'd been classmates in Debrecen, he "believed me" but he had no memory of it, which I found quite interesting! Another school friend who returned from the camps was Gyuri Gergely. I remained in touch with him and he visited us in Canada twice. He was a journalist in Budapest.[4] Gabi Horovitz survived the war and the deportation and went to live in Israel, where he became the director of an agricultural institute. My friend Gyuri Kemény did become a writer, and he was the dramaturge for one of Budapest's theatres. He had some kind of a run-in with his boss and consequently fell afoul of the Communist regime. He didn't see a way out of the situation and ended his life by suicide.[5]

Going back to Hungary after the deportation, we too started a new life. To have survived the war was a miracle. We were alive. We were free. We could decide the direction of our future; the coming years had to be decisive because our first steps needed to take us toward a happy life.

---

4 György Gergely (1925–2008) was trained as a glazier after the war. He became a chair of the glassworkers' association and also a journalist at the craftsmen's journal.

5 György Kemény (1928–1972) was a journalist, literary critic and dramaturge of the Thália Theatre in Budapest.

The subsequent eleven years, between 1945 and 1956, were busy. During this time, I got my Mechanical Engineering diploma at the Technical University of Budapest and spent seven years as a plant engineer at the Láng Machine Factory. Gyuri and I grew really close to each other when we returned from the deportation. I moved to Budapest to attend the Technical University, while he stayed at home to help our parents. That's how I could study without interference, later having a good job and starting a family. I loved my parents, but Gyuri was capable of making any sacrifice on their behalf. Gyuri later wanted to go to Palestine. He had gotten as far as Italy when I wrote to him to say how much the family needed him in Debrecen, so he returned home and resumed supporting our parents, helping Father in the new leather store in Debrecen so that they could earn a living. Gyuri, the overlooked younger brother, became a giant in our eyes; he became the family's guardian angel and enabled me to finish my engineering studies. Later, he came to Budapest. He graduated from business college and got a job at the National Hungarian Tourism Agency. By that time, we had common friends and grew even closer.

Then everything fell apart. Everything. Gyuri got married in 1954, and half a year later, in January 1955, he died. The cancer finished him off in four weeks; at least he didn't suffer much. Tragically, he and my father died within a week of one another. But we spared them each the pain of knowing about the other's death. My mother lost her husband and her beloved little son at the same time. And that finished her life as well. When she later came with us to Canada, she was quite ill; she had Parkinson's disease, and her health deteriorated rapidly. Although she lived with us, it felt like she was waiting to be with them, and eleven years after losing her husband and son, she passed away at seventy years old. If there is an afterlife, my brother is there by our parents' side, taking care of them. And he will also take care of me if I get to join them.

For a very long time, I couldn't accept that I did not have a brother anymore. I'm not religious, and I'm hardly superstitious, but somehow I cannot imagine never being reunited with my first family. There's an English saying about love being what binds two people together, and this bond will remain even when one of them is no longer alive. The bond between my parents, my brother and me is probably stronger now than when they were alive. I feel that everything that I am, and what I have become, I owe to them. I am as well a link in the chain between the ancestors and the descendants, with whom I share a bond that's also strong but different. I feel that everything they are and what they have become, they owe to me as well. My first family was responsible for me and I became responsible for my second family. It is gratitude that binds me to my first family and devotion to the second one, and my inextinguishable love for both of them.

In 1949, I married Judy, who shared our deportation years. We created a home and we had two great boys, Peter and George, and learned to be parents. However, after the first promising years it was difficult to exist in a Communist country, which became ever darker and more oppressive, more dangerous.

By a new miracle, for a short time, emigration opened up. In 1956, we immigrated to Canada.[6] It was a momentous step, as decisive as surviving the deportation. Our family's future turned in a new direction in its long wandering and it was difficult because we were not prepared. Being an engineer helped, but not too much. I had to learn that being an engineer here in Canada didn't mean being in the shop organizing and directing the production, but working in an office instead. After three months, however, I figured it out and from this point, Canada opened up for me.

After the suppression of the 1956 anti-communist and anti-Soviet revolt, some two hundred thousand people, mostly from the urban middle class and the youth, left Hungary for the west, mostly Great Britain, the United States and Canada. At least one-fifth of this cohort were Jews, who were motivated by economic and political reasons, as well as by the fear of another wave of antisemitic violence.

I started as a draftsman and two and a half years was enough for me to learn English and take a course in computer programming at the University of Toronto. After that I could get a job in a management consulting company. First I was a programmer, then a systems analyst and a consultant for the companies who used my programs. Our company, KCS Ltd., later merged to become Kates, Peat, Marwick & Co. In 1968, the Ministry of Health was looking for people to introduce OHIP in Ontario, and I was hired with other people to organize and program OHIP. I spent twenty years with the Ministry of Health, from which I retired in 1988.

My wife, Judy, who was a photographer in Hungary, worked with Toronto's Horvath Photography, a well-known studio. She was the retoucher, responsible for dealing with the customers and many of their photos.

Peter, who turned sixty-five, has been married now for many years and lives in Long Island, New York. He works as a principal engineer in a bar-code reader manufacturing company. No children, no population explosion.

George — what a coincidence — is a professional engineer as well. He has been a chemical engineer at Rothmans International (now Rothmans, Benson & Hedges) since 1978. He is married with two sons — the eldest, Thomas (Tommy), is an actuary with Sun Life Financial and is married with two children: a lovely little girl, Mackenzie, and a two-year-old son, Lincoln; Andrew, the youngest, is still in school and will finish soon.

Judy and I are happily retired and have been together for more than seventy years. In all the time we have been in Canada, it has changed as well. Our country became a role model for many countries as a safe and peaceful place, where it is good to live. Hungary was not good to us. It always discriminated against us because we were Jews and ultimately it delivered us to our murderers. Canada made up for all this and we have to be grateful for it. Here we could live a full and meaningful life. We couldn't have hoped for more than that. It is a life worth living.

After liberation and my return to Hungary, I stopped keeping a diary for a long time. I was busy starting a new life. From that period, all I have left is my letters addressed to Judit. In January 1955, after losing both my father and my brother within one week, I returned to writing again.

In May 1955, I restarted my diary — my life. I have an entry for almost every day, which I have done for more than sixty years. There is a notebook for each year — many, many notebooks carefully lined up on my desk. They are all written in Hungarian, except for the diary of my deportation, which has been translated into English.

As far back as I can remember, I always kept a diary. When I thought that something important had happened to me, I would write it down. I used to record my thoughts in a separate notebook. All my pre-war notebooks got lost in the conflagration. Here in Canada I marvelled at the fact that objects survived many generations and were handed down from parents to children. There is no break in continuity. My grandson inherits my son's teddy bear. Photos of my son's childhood are looked at by his sons. Things from thirty-five years ago still exist — the buildings where we once lived, our furniture, the books.

All that was left from my father was a small pocket knife, and from my mother, a worn-out handbag in which she kept a note with the anniversary dates of my father's and brother's deaths according to the Jewish calendar, but our Hungarian past is otherwise mostly gone without a trace. The last house we lived in before the deportation, 14 Vörösmarty Street, does not exist anymore, and no other physical trace of our lives remains either. Only the memories.

Here in Canada there is continuity, an unbroken sequence passing from father to son, from son to grandson. There, my youth was brought to an end by the war and deportation. There, my adulthood was interrupted by emigration, after which a whole new life started. From that point on, everything that had happened in Hungary became history. Not just personal history, but the history of the whole family. After Spain, Turkey and Hungary, my family will continue in Canada and that's how the story of my life becomes a turning point in my family's history.

If a misguided bomb had killed me, or the SS soldiers had shot me with their machine guns, if I had perished in this war along with millions of other victims, I would not have been the only one who had died. My sons, Peter and George, wouldn't be here either, and neither would Thomas and Andrew, our grandchildren, nor all those who will follow them.

The long chain of my ancestors that takes me back uncountable millennia would have been broken. My forefathers who had to flee from country to country, who were hiding and suffered terrible fates to save their lives, and thereby also mine, would have suffered in vain.

But they didn't suffer in vain. They prevailed over their persecutors. I hope for yet many more generations. Amen.

Epilogue

I would like to end this memoir with one of my diary entries from 2005.

January 27, 2005, was the sixtieth anniversary of the liberation of Auschwitz by the Red Army. The leaders of the world took a pilgrimage to this terrible place where the Nazis slaughtered one and a half million people without any reason. Three heads of states — Russian, Polish and Israeli — spoke.[1] Then the shofar was blown and there was a short prayer.

This vast graveyard is covered with the dust of one and a half million men, women and children. The wind stirs and lifts this holy dust and scatters it all over the world. It flies everywhere. It settles everywhere. We breathe it in. Each one of us carries it. Our children will carry it and our grandchildren will carry it. They lodge, the million and a half, in our bodies. They are part of us. They are part of all humanity. The sun will shine on them for ever and ever.

The audience of more than five hundred included twenty-five heads of state, and both US vice-president Dick Cheney and Ukrainian president Victor Yushchenko spoke as well, as did a number of dignitaries and Holocaust survivors.

Glossary

Auschwitz (German; in Polish, Oświęcim) A Nazi concentration camp complex in German-occupied Poland about 50 kilometres from Krakow, on the outskirts of the town of Oświęcim, built between 1940 and 1942. The largest camp complex established by the Nazis, Auschwitz contained three main camps: Auschwitz I, a concentration camp; Auschwitz II (Birkenau), a death camp that used gas chambers to commit mass murder; and Auschwitz III (also called Monowitz or Buna), which provided slave labour for an industrial complex. In 1942, the Nazis began to deport Jews from almost every country in Europe to Auschwitz-Birkenau, where they were selected for slave labour or for death in the gas chambers. Starting in May 1944, over 420,000 Hungarian Jews were deported to Auschwitz-Birkenau in mass transports, with smaller groups arriving through October 1944. The majority of these Jews were killed immediately in the gas chambers. In mid-January 1945, close to 60,000 inmates were sent on a death march, leaving behind only a few thousand inmates who were liberated by the Soviet army on January 27, 1945. It is estimated that 1.1 million people were murdered in Auschwitz, approximately 90 per cent of whom were Jewish; other victims included Polish prisoners, Roma and Soviet prisoners of war. *See also* Birkenau.

bar mitzvah (Hebrew; son of the commandment) The time when, in Jewish tradition, boys become religiously and morally responsible for their actions and are considered adults for the purpose of synagogue and other rituals. Traditionally this occurs at age thirteen for boys. A bar mitzvah is also the synagogue ceremony and family celebration that marks the attainment of this status, during which the bar mitzvah boy is called upon to read a portion of the Torah and recite the prescribed prayers in a public prayer service.

Birkenau Also known as Auschwitz II. One of the camps in the Auschwitz complex in German-occupied Poland and the largest death camp established by the Nazis. Birkenau was built in 1941, and in 1942 the Nazis designated it as a killing centre, using Zyklon B gas to carry out the systematic murder of Jews and other people considered "undesirable" by the Nazis. In 1943, the Nazis began to use four crematoria with gas chambers that could hold up to 2,000 people each to murder the large numbers of Jews who were being brought to the camp from across Europe. Upon arrival, prisoners were selected for slave labour or sent to the gas chambers. The camp was liberated in January 1945 by the Soviet army. An estimated 1.1 million people were killed in the Auschwitz camp complex, most of them in Birkenau and the vast majority of them Jews. *See also* Auschwitz.

bochur A young unmarried boy or man, specifically a student of Jewish studies.

British Mandate Palestine (also Mandatory Palestine) The area of the Middle East under British rule from 1923 to 1948 comprising present-day Israel, Jordan, the West Bank and the Gaza Strip. The Mandate was established by the League of Nations after World War I and the collapse of the Ottoman Empire; the area was given to the British to administer until a Jewish national home could be established. During this time, Jewish immigration was severely restricted, and Jews and Arabs clashed with the British and each other as they struggled to realize their national interests. The

Mandate ended on May 15, 1948, after the United Nations Partition Plan for Palestine was adopted and on the same day that the State of Israel was declared.

Budapest ghetto The area of Budapest in which Jews were confined, established by Hungary's Arrow Cross government on November 29, 1944. On December 10, the ghetto was sealed off from the rest of the city. Jews under the protection of neutral states were first moved into a separate, smaller ghetto known as the international ghetto, but most of them were soon transferred into the main, larger one. By early January 1945, the population of the overcrowded ghetto reached close to 70,000, and people lacked sufficient food, water and sanitation. Supplies dwindled and conditions worsened during the Soviet siege of Budapest, which began in late December 1944. Thousands died of starvation and disease. The ghetto was also vulnerable to Arrow Cross raids, and thousands of Jews were taken from the ghetto and murdered on the banks of the Danube. Soviet forces liberated the short-lived ghetto between January 16 and 18, 1945. *See also* ghetto.

cholent (Yiddish) A traditional Jewish stew usually prepared on Friday and slow-cooked overnight to be eaten for Shabbat (the Sabbath) lunch. Ingredients for cholent vary by geographic region, but usually include meat, potatoes, beans and a grain.

ghetto A confined residential area for Jews. The term originated in Venice, Italy, in 1516 with a law requiring all Jews to live on a segregated, gated island known as Ghetto Nuovo. Throughout the Middle Ages in Europe, Jews were often forcibly confined to gated Jewish neighbourhoods. Beginning in 1939, the Nazis forced Jews to live in crowded and unsanitary conditions in designated areas — usually the poorest ones — of cities and towns in Eastern Europe. Ghettos were often enclosed by walls and gates, and entry and exit from the ghettos were strictly controlled. Family and community life continued to some degree, but starvation and disease were rampant. Starting in 1941, the ghettos were liquidated, and Jews were deported to camps and killing centres.

Gobelin A specific style of a tapestry, named for a historic family of weavers from France.

Havdalah (Hebrew; separation) A Jewish ritual done at the end of the Sabbath and Jewish holidays, marking the separation between days of holiness and ordinary weekdays. During the Havdalah after the Sabbath, blessings are recited over a cup of wine, fragrant spices and a candle flame. *See also* Sabbath.

kosher (Hebrew) Fit to eat according to Jewish dietary laws. Observant Jews follow a system of rules known as *kashruth* that regulates what can be eaten, how food is prepared and how animals are slaughtered. Food is kosher when it has been deemed fit for consumption according to this system of rules. There are several foods that are forbidden, most notably pork products and shellfish.

labour service (Also referred to as forced labour battalions; in Hungarian, *Munkaszolgálat*) Units of Hungary's military-related labour service system, which was established for Hungarians considered too "politically unreliable" for regular military service. After the labour service was made compulsory in 1939, Jewish men of military age were recruited to serve; however, having been deemed "unfit" to bear arms, they were equipped with tools and employed in mining, road and rail construction and maintenance work. Though the men were treated relatively well at first, the system became increasingly punitive. By 1941, Jews in forced labour battalions were required to wear an armband and civilian clothes; they had no formal rank and were unarmed; they were often mistreated by extremely antisemitic supervisors; and the work they had to do, such as clearing minefields, was often fatal. By 1942, 100,000 Jewish men had been drafted into labour battalions, and by the time the Germans occupied Hungary in March 1944, between 25,000 and 40,000 Hungarian Jewish men had died during their forced labour service.

Lager (German) Camp.

Maftir The last portion of the weekly Torah reading chanted in the synagogue on Shabbat and holidays; the person called up to the Torah for the Maftir portion then chants the weekly reading from the prophets, the Haftarah.

Mishnah (Hebrew; learning through repetition) The oral traditions of Jewish law compiled around 200 CE and arranged by subject. This text serves as the basis of later rabbinic studies and commentaries on Jewish law.

Nazi camps The roughly 20,000 prison camps established by the Nazis between 1933 and 1945. Although the term "concentration camp" is often used to refer generally to all these facilities, the various camps had a wide variety of functions. They included concentration camps; forced labour camps; prisoner-of-war (POW) camps; transit camps; and death camps. Concentration camps were detention facilities first built in 1933 to imprison "enemies of the state," while forced labour camps held prisoners who had to do hard physical labour under brutal working conditions. POW camps were designated for captured prisoners of war, and transit camps operated as holding facilities for Jews who were to be transported to other camps — often death camps in Poland. Death camps — including Auschwitz-Birkenau, Belzec, Chelmno, Sobibor and Treblinka — were killing centres where designated groups of people were murdered on a highly organized, mass scale. Some camps, such as Majdanek, combined several of these functions.

Orthodox Judaism The religious practice of Jews for whom the observance of Judaism is rooted in the traditional rabbinical interpretations of the biblical commandments. Orthodox Jewish practice is characterized by strict observance of Jewish law and tradition, such as the prohibition to work on the Sabbath and certain dietary restrictions.

Ostarbeiter (German; Eastern workers) Soviet and Polish slave labourers, mostly Ukrainians, who were forced to work to supply labour for the German war effort during World War II.

partisan A member of an irregular military force or resistance movement formed to oppose armies of occupation. During World War
II there were a number of different partisan groups that opposed
the Nazis and their collaborators in several countries. The term
partisan could include highly organized, almost paramilitary
groups such as the Red Army partisans; ad hoc groups bent more
on survival than resistance; and roving groups of bandits who
plundered what they could from all sides during the war.

Red Cross A humanitarian organization founded in 1863 to protect
the victims of war. During World War II, the Red Cross provided
assistance to prisoners of war by distributing food parcels and
monitoring the situation in POW camps and also provided medical attention to wounded soldiers and civilians. Today, in addition
to the international body, the International Committee of the Red
Cross (ICRC), there are national Red Cross and Red Crescent so-
cieties in almost every country in the world.

Roma (singular male, Rom; singular female, Romni) A traditionally
itinerant ethnic group originally from northern India and primarily located in Central and Eastern Europe. The Roma, who
have been referred to pejoratively as Gypsies, have often lived on
the fringes of society and been subject to persecution. During the
Holocaust, which the Roma refer to as the Porajmos — the destruction or devouring — Roma were stripped of their citizenship
under the Nuremberg Laws and were targeted for death under
Hitler's race policies. It is estimated that between 220,000 and
500,000 Roma were murdered in the Holocaust. Roma Holocaust
Memorial Day is commemorated on August 2.

Rosh Hashanah (Hebrew; New Year) The two-day autumn holiday that marks the beginning of the Jewish year and ushers in
the High Holy Days. It is celebrated with a prayer service and the
blowing of the shofar (ram's horn), as well as festive meals that
include symbolic foods such as an apple dipped in honey, which
symbolizes the desire for a sweet new year.

Sabbath (in Hebrew, Shabbat; in Yiddish, Shabbes, Shabbos) The weekly day of rest beginning Friday at sunset and ending Saturday at nightfall, ushered in by the lighting of candles on Friday evening and the recitation of blessings over wine and challah (egg bread). A day of celebration as well as prayer, it is customary to eat three festive meals, attend synagogue services and refrain from doing any work or travelling.

Shema Yisrael (Hebrew; also Shema; Hear, O Israel) An important Jewish prayer comprising three paragraphs of biblical verses. The prayer starts with the verse "Hear, O Israel: the Lord is our God, the Lord is one." The Shema, or parts of it, is recited in various prayer services. It is considered a fundamental expression of faith in God, and its opening verse is sometimes spoken by Jews as a prayer of supplication and when facing death.

shnoder (Yiddish; from the Hebrew "shenadar," "who promises"; in Hungarian, *snóder*) A pledge to make a donation, given when one is called up to the Torah.

SS (abbreviation of Schutzstaffel; Defence Corps) The elite police force of the Nazi regime that was responsible for security and for the enforcement of Nazi racial policies, including the implementation of the "Final Solution" — a euphemistic term referring to the Nazis' plan to systematically murder Europe's Jewish population. The SS was established in 1925 as Adolf Hitler's elite bodyguard unit, and under the direction of Heinrich Himmler, its membership grew from 280 in 1929 to 52,000 when the Nazis came to power in 1933, and to nearly a quarter of a million on the eve of World War II. SS recruits were screened for their racial purity and had to prove their "Aryan" lineage. The SS ran the concentration and death camps and also established the Waffen-SS, its own military division that was independent of the German army.

tallis (Yiddish; in Hebrew, *tallit*; prayer shawl) A four-cornered ritual garment that is draped over the shoulders or head, traditionally worn by Jewish men during morning prayers and on the

Day of Atonement (Yom Kippur). Fringes on the four corners of the garment are meant to remind the wearer to fulfill the biblical commandments.

tefillin (Hebrew; phylacteries) A pair of black leather boxes containing scrolls of parchment inscribed with Bible verses and traditionally worn by Jewish men on the arm and forehead at prescribed times of prayer as a symbol of the covenantal relationship with God.

Theresienstadt (German; in Czech, Terezín) A walled town in the Czech Republic sixty kilometres north of Prague that served as a ghetto, a transit camp and a concentration camp. Despite the terrible living conditions in the ghetto, a rich cultural life developed that included artistic performances, clandestine schools and a vast lending library. The Nazis showcased Theresienstadt as a model ghetto for propaganda purposes, to demonstrate to delegates from the International Red Cross and others their supposedly humane treatment of Jews and to counter information reaching the Allies about Nazi atrocities and mass murder. In total, approximately 140,000 Jews were deported to Theresienstadt between 1941 and 1945. About 33,000 prisoners died in Theresienstadt, and nearly 90,000 others were sent on to death camps, including Auschwitz-Birkenau. The Soviet army liberated the remaining prisoners on May 9, 1945.

Warsaw Ghetto Uprising A large rebellion by Jewish resistance fighters in the Warsaw ghetto, beginning on April 19, 1943, and lasting several weeks. After the mass deportation and murder of ghetto inhabitants in the summer of 1942, resistance groups prepared for an uprising. In January 1943, the Nazis attempted to deport the remaining Jews, but they encountered armed resistance and suspended deportations. When the Nazis entered the ghetto to deport the remaining inhabitants in April 1943, about 750 organized ghetto fighters launched an insurrection, while the other inhabitants took shelter in hiding places and underground bunkers. The resistance fighters were defeated on May 16, 1943, resulting in the destruction of the ghetto and the deportation of the remaining Jews; more than 56,000 Jews were captured and deported, and about 7,000 were shot.

Yom Kippur (Hebrew; Day of Atonement) A solemn day of fasting and repentance that comes eight days after Rosh Hashanah, the Jewish New Year, and marks the end of the High Holidays.

Zionism A movement promoted by the Viennese Jewish journalist Theodor Herzl, who argued in his 1896 book *Der Judenstaat* (The Jewish State) that the best way to resolve the problem of antisemitism and persecution of Jews in Europe was to create an independent Jewish state in the historical Jewish homeland of biblical Israel. Zionists also promoted the revival of Hebrew as a Jewish national language.

Photographs

1 Leslie's maternal grandfather, Josef Deutsch.
2 Leslie's maternal great-grandmother (left), name unknown, and his grandmother, Kathleen (Kati).
3 Leslie's mother, Flora Deutsch, before the war. Hungary, date unknown.
4 Leslie's father, Andor Frenkel, before the war. Hungary, date unknown.

1 Leslie at around age five with his younger brother, Gyuri (George) at age one. Debrecen, Hungary, circa 1930.

2 Leslie with his mother. Debrecen, Hungary, circa 1935.

3 Leslie at eighteen years old, after matriculating from high school. Debrecen, Hungary, 1943.

The ghetto in Debrecen, Hungary, 1944, showing the wooden fence of the ghetto in Simonffy Street. In the background is the building of the Jewish Gymnasium. Photo credit: Hungarian National Museum.

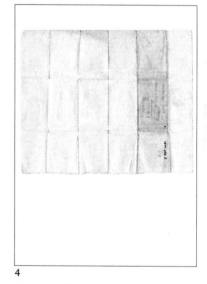

1 & 2 The first letter that Judy was able to send Leslie while they were both working as forced labourers in different districts of Vienna, Austria. September 25, 1944.

3 & 4 The first letter written by Leslie that was delivered to Judy. October 8, 1944.

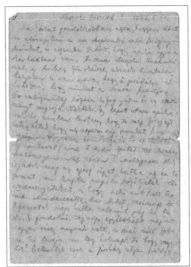

1 & 2 The last letter that Leslie was able to send to Judy. February 2, 1945. The names "Sarah" and "Izrael" had to precede Judy's and Leslie's names as per Nazi regulations for Jews.

3 & 4 Judy's last letter to Leslie. March 20, 1945.

1 Leslie (left) with Judy (centre), his brother, George (right), and their parents, Flora and Andor (in front), after the war. Debrecen, Hungary, circa 1948.

2 Leslie's brother, George. Budapest, Hungary, circa 1950.

3 Leslie in Debrecen, circa 1948.

1

2

3

1–3 Leslie and Judy after the war. Debrecen, Hungary, circa 1947.

1–3 Leslie and Judy. Hungary, circa 1948.

1 Leslie and Judy, circa 1948.
2 Leslie and Judy. Toronto, circa 2010.

1 Leslie's son Peter and Peter's wife, Vicky.
2 Leslie's son George and George's wife, Diane.
3 Leslie with his grandsons Tom (left) and Andrew (right) as teenagers.
4 Leslie with Andrew (left) and Tom (right) as young men.

1 Leslie and family at the wedding of his grandson Tom to Olivia. From left to right
   (in back): Leslie's grandson Andrew; Leslie's son George; Olivia; Tom; Leslie;
   Leslie's son Peter and Peter's wife, Vicky. In front, Diane and Judy (right).
2 Leslie's great-grandchildren, Lincoln and Mackenzie.

Leslie Fazekas, 2015.

Index

Floridsdorf, xxxii, 42, 53*n*48, 70,
71, 74
food: at Aspern camp, 29–30; at
Floridsdorf, 42; in Frenkel family home, 86, 102; prisoners talking about, 8*n*12; at Saurerwerke
camp, 5, 11, 12, 19–20, 27; stashes,
13, 31, 115; supplies, xxiv, xxxi
forced labour: agricultural, xxxi,
28–29; auxiliary army, xxii; fit-
ness for work, 63; rubble-clear-
ing, xxxii, 42. *See also* labour
service
Frank, András (Janka), 46
Frenkel, Andor (father): businesses
and education, 82–83, 108; factory work and labour camp, 26;
family life, 89; final years, 124;
in hospital, 49, 51, 56, 66–67, 74;
illnesses, 47, 48, 115; in labour
service, 109; personality and
habits, 83–84, 102; reuniting
with family, 121; and transfer
request, 57, 66
Frenkel, Ferenc (uncle), 121
Frenkel, Flora (mother, née
Deutsch): in danger, 120; final
years, 124; illness and recovery,
9, 11, 12, 15; László compliments,
88; life at camp, 65, 68, 114–115;
personality and habits, 84, 86
Frenkel, Gyuri (George, brother):
at labour camp, 26, 65, 68, 114;
final years, 124; relationship
with László, 83, 86, 101; reuniting with father, 121; on return to

Debrecen, 120
Frenkel, József and Aranka (grandparents), 91, 113
Frenkel, László (Leslie Fazekas,
also Gazsi, Laci): activities in
childhood, 89–90, 93–94; books
and reading, 88, 92–93, 101, 105;
conversations with father, 83–84;
diary writing, 4, 33, 79–80, 116,
127; first memories, 81–82; and
Gyuri, 101, 124; interests, 88–89,
103, 107; labour service, 109–110;
marriage, family, and life in
Canada, 125–126; newspaper
job, 121; religion and beliefs, 80,
96–97; retrospection of Lager
life, 79–80; school, 87–88; social
life, 103–104, 105, 107–108; studies and career direction, 15, 80,
102–103, 108, 124; violin lessons,
85; visits with relatives, 92–94,
99–101
— AT LABOUR CAMP: air-raid
experiences, 21–22; barracks
move, 54; birthday plans, 6,
14–15; concerns about studies, 3,
5, 13, 25, 45; decision to escape,
117–118; factory work, 24–26, 31,
37, 48, 51, 69; and fellow prisoners, 4, 26–27, 31, 37; losing ability
to think, 22–23; New Year's Eve
reflections, 44–46; no one to
talk to, 1, 19; planning for transfer, 57; "preparing to die," 58–59,
63–64; schedules and routines,
8, 48–49, 75

Szeged deportees, xix

Szemere, Tamás (Tomi), 46, 103–104

Szolnok deportees, xix

teachers, 105–106

Teitelbaum, Dezső (uncle), 99, 120, 122

Teitelbaum, Leslie (cousin), 99, 120, 122

Teitelbaum, Márta (cousin), 99–100, 122

Teitelbaum, Szerén (aunt), 99, 120, 122

Theresienstadt, 71n59, 74

Törökszentmiklós, 92–93

The Tragedy of Man (Madách), 35

train transports, xxv–xxvi, 112

transit camps: decision-making at, xxvi–xxvii. *See also* Strasshof transit camp

Tuchmann, Dr. Emil, xxxii, 57, 61

Two Prisoners (Zilahy), 3

Ujhel (Sátoraljaújhely), 92, 93–94

University of Debrecen, 108

Varga, Béla, xxxi$n$17

Vaszary, Gábor (writer), 101

Vienna and districts, xvi, xxxii, xxxiii, xxxviii, 120. *See also* Floridsdorf; Simmering

Waltner (hospital patient), 20, 24

war news, 106–107

war veterans, 90–91

water supplies, xxiv, 59, 113, 119

Weiszman, Zoltán, 106

woman from Vienna (Red Cross visitor), 12, 13, 15, 116

Yom Kippur (Day of Atonement), 14–15

Zionism, xvii–xviii, 97n14

The Azrieli Foundation was established in 1989 to realize and extend the philanthropic vision of David J. Azrieli, C.M., C.Q., M.Arch. The Foundation's mission is to support a wide spectrum of initiatives in education and research. The Azrieli Foundation is an active supporter of programs in the fields of education, the education of architects, scientific and medical research, and the arts. The Azrieli Foundation's many initiatives include: the Holocaust Survivor Memoirs Program, which collects, preserves, publishes and distributes the written memoirs of survivors in Canada; the Azrieli Institute for Educational Empowerment, an innovative program successfully working to keep at-risk youth in school; the Azrieli Fellows Program, which promotes academic excellence and leadership on the graduate level at Israeli universities; the Azrieli Music Project, which celebrates and fosters the creation of high-quality new Jewish orchestral music; and the Azrieli Neurodevelopmental Research Program, which supports advanced research on neurodevelopmental disorders, particularly Fragile X and Autism Spectrum Disorders.